William Cornelius Wyckoff

Silk Manufacture in the United States

William Cornelius Wyckoff

Silk Manufacture in the United States

ISBN/EAN: 9783743310001

Manufactured in Europe, USA, Canada, Australia, Japa

Cover: Foto ©ninafisch / pixelio.de

Manufactured and distributed by brebook publishing software (www.brebook.com)

William Cornelius Wyckoff

Silk Manufacture in the United States

SILK MANUFACTURE

IN THE

UNITED STATES.

BY

WM. C. WYCKOFF,

(Secretary of the Silk Association of America).

PUBLISHED AND FOR SALE AT

446 BROOME STREET,

NEW YORK.

1883.

PREFACE.

A very small number of copies has been issued at Washington, of the Report to the Census of 1880, on the Silk Manufacturing Industry of the United States. The Report is here reproduced in a more convenient form, to meet a demand for its wider circulation.

The historical sketch of attempts in Silk Culture, beginning with the earliest settlements in this country, will, it is believed, be found of special interest at the present time. The Tenth Annual Report of the Silk Association of America supplies statistics of manufacture and import to a later date than the census. The Directory of Silk Manufacturers is compiled from new returns, showing the most recent changes of firms and addresses.

W. C. W.

November, 1882.

CONTENTS.

	PAGE.
History of the Silk Industry	5
Census Statistics of the Industry, to 1880	54
Index to History and Census Statistics	65
Tenth Annual Report, Silk Association of America	75
Statistics of Tenth Annual Report	91
Directory of American Silk Manufacture	107
Directory of Raw Silk Importers and Brokers	139
Business Announcements	141

REPORT

ON THE

SILK MANUFACTURING

→∗INDUSTRY∗←

OF THE

UNITED STATES.

COMPILED BY

WM. C. WYCKOFF,

SPECIAL AGENT FOR THE

TENTH CENSUS OF THE UNITED STATES.

LETTER OF TRANSMITTAL.

NEW YORK, N. Y., *October* 7, 1881.

Hon. FRANCIS A. WALKER,
Superintendent of Census, Washington, D. C.

DEAR SIR:—I have the honor to submit herewith a report upon the silk manufactures of the United States. The report covers the entire period from the earliest introduction of silk into America to June 30, 1880. I am under obligations, which I take great pleasure in acknowledging, for assistance in the historical references, to Mr. J. Carson Brevoort, of Brooklyn, to the Long Island Historical Society, and to the Society Library of New York; and for efficient aid, in the statistical portion of the work, to Mr. P. T. Wood, of New Providence, New Jersey. In closing my labors I embrace the opportunity to express my hearty thanks for the uniform promptness and courtesy of your office at Washington.

Yours respectfully,

WM. C. WYCKOFF,

Special Agent.

SILK MANUFACTURE.

The Spanish conquest of Mexico was the means of introducing the silk industry on this continent. We may dismiss the vexed question alluded to by Prescott (a) as to whether the Aztecs made fabrics containing silk. Humboldt declares that the material they used was not the product of the *Bombyx mori*. (b) Herrera asserts that there was no silk, (c) and Acosta, that there were no mulberry trees in the Indies prior to their introduction from Spain. The voluminous work of Hernandez (d) gives full accounts of the plants and animals of the new world, and does not mention the silkworm or the mulberry.

In the year 1522, Cortes, as ruler of New Spain (Mexico) prepared a plan for its government; the details included the appointment of officials in charge of the silk industry. The first step was the planting of mulberry trees, and we learn that these were flourishing near the city of Mexico a few years afterward. The record of certain legal proceedings has secured to history the date of the introduction of the silkworm into America. After Cortes withdrew from personal rule in New Spain, the authorities who were placed in charge by the king made an investigation of what had been done by the board of auditors who preceded them. This was in the year 1531. Among the items of this procedure is a statement (e) that a quarter of an ounce of silkworm seed (eggs) was sent on public account from Spain to Francisco de Santa Cruz, a citizen of Mexico. The seed arrived in safety, and was placed by Francisco with Auditor Diego Delgadillo, who was a native of Granada, and presumably knew something of silk culture in his own country, where it was introduced by the Moors. Delgadillo made use of the eggs in a garden about a league from the capital, where mulberry trees were in good condition for the support of the worms. The experiment was eminently successful. The auditor returned two ounces

---

a Conquest of Mexico, vol. i, p. 144; note.

b Essai Politique, book v, chap. 12.

c Historia General, decade v, book vi, chap. 12.

d Rerum Medicarum Novæ Hispaniæ Thesaurus (Rome. 1651), first published in 1607.

e Historia General, decade iv, book ix, chap. 4. Also, Descripcion, chap. x.

of eggs to Francisco, and retained enough to supply various amounts to other people. The point of the accusation against Delgadillo was that he sold this seed at $60 per ounce; thus disposing of the property of the crown for his own benefit. He was convicted of the crime, though credited with the introduction of silk into the country.

This was the beginning of an industry in the culture of silk, its manufacture into woven goods, and their export abroad, which has not generally attracted the notice of modern writers on the subject. Acosta gives the following account:

> But the silke that is made in New Spaine is transported into other countries, as to Peru. There were no mulberrie trees in the Indies but such as were brought from Spaine, and they grow well, especially in the province which they call Mistecqua, where there are silkwormes, and they put to worke the silke they gather, whereof they make very good taffetaes: Yet to this day they have made neyther damaske, sattin nor velvet. (*a*)

By the end of the sixteenth century this manufacture had almost wholly ceased. (*b*)

So far as silk culture is concerned, however, the industry was after a short interval to reappear on this continent, and unfold itself in the sunshine of royal favor. A brief reference to European events may throw light on the causes that brought about the new effort. At the beginning of the seventeenth century Henry IV, of France, was at the height of his glory and power. Olivier de Serres, whom the French call "the father of agriculture", published in the year 1600 an important and suggestive book on field husbandry. The work attracted the attention of the king, and he bestowed high honor and authority upon its author. Upon the recommendation of de Serres, 14,000 mulberry trees were brought from Italy and planted in the royal gardens of France. Shortly afterward silkworm eggs were similarly procured, and other measures were taken to encourage the nascent manufacture. The prime minister of the king looked coldly upon this enterprise. An old and respectable citizen, the spokesman of a deputation from the silk merchants of Paris, was at this time treated with extreme rudeness by Sully. The quaint garb of the merchant, ornamented with various silks, was made the subject of mockery; the old man, while on his knees to the great minister, was twirled around and dismissed with a sneer. Returning to his friends, the merchant reported that the servant was above his

---

a The Naturall and Morall Historie of the East and West Indies, by Joseph de Acosta, book iv, chap. 32. Edwd. Grimestone's transl.; London, 1604.

b Essai Politique, Humboldt, book v, chap. 12.

master. Never was there a greater mistake. The king had a will of his own, and was about to help the silk merchants of France toward a prosperity far beyond their dreams. Sully tells the story of his own discomfiture. (*a*) "I exclaimed against this project, which I never liked; but the king was prepossessed; all that I could say was futile." In vain the minister argued that luxury should be repressed, most certainly not encouraged. "I could not persuade him. 'Are these,' he said to me, 'the good reasons you have to offer? I would much rather fight the king of Spain in three pitched battles than all those gentlemen of the robe, of the inkstand, and of the city, beside their wives and daughters, whom you will bring down upon me with your fantastic regulations.'"

The industry was established in France and made notable progress, as to both culture and manufacture. It soon excited the envy of (*b*) James I of England, and he proceeded to copy, even in details, the performance of Henry of Navarre. So the royal gardens at Oatlands were stocked with mulberry trees and the worms were fed on English soil. In 1608 King James addressed a long letter on the subject, written with his own hand, to the lords-lieutenant of every county in his kingdom. He orders that they shall "persuade and require such as are of ability to buy and distribute in your county the number of ten thousand mulberry plants, which shall be delivered to them at the rate of three farthings the plant, or at six shillings the hundred". (*c*) Mulberry seeds were to be furnished also in the following spring, and to be similarly distributed, *i. e.*, at a price. The supposed wants of England having received attention, America was next looked after. In fact, however, nearly a century elapsed after their introduction by the Spaniards before silkworm eggs were again brought to this continent from Europe, and King James supplied the "seed". The undertaking met with delay at the outset. The expedition of Sir George Summers with a fleet of seven vessels bound for the shores of Virginia in 1609, suffered shipwreck and disaster. Two vessels were lost entirely; the rest were driven by storm to the Bermudas. A part of the expedition ultimately reached Virginia, but brought no silkworm eggs. This was two years after the settlement of Jamestown (named in honor of the king) by the London Company, the holders of a grant which covered the region between 34° and 41° of latitude. There is abundant evi-

---

a Mémoires de Sully, année 1603, liv. xvi; London, 1778, vol. v, pp. 150-159.
b An Essay upon the Silk-Worm, by Henry Barham; London, 1719, p. 46.
c *Ibid.*, p. 50. This letter was printed with "Instructions for the Increasing of Mulberrie Trees and the Breeding of Silke-Worms" (illust.), London; 1609.

dence that the colonists were in no condition at this period to prosecute silk culture. Indeed they were soon afterward on the verge of starvation.

The historian of the unlucky voyage of 1609, William Strachy, seems to have taken much interest in silk. He mentions that they found silkworms on the Bermuda islands rolled up in the leaves of the palmetto, and that these worms were like those described by Acosta, that were found on the *tunall* tree. The two statements are bewildering errors, and it is worth while to notice them as of a piece with many records of native silkworms found in the Bermudas and on the American continent. The true silkworm does not roll itself in palmetto leaves. Acosta had evidently not seen the "worms" he refers to; his description of the cactus on which they feed and the red dye that is obtained from them, shows that he was giving an account on hearsay, being very imperfectly informed, respecting the cochineal insect. No doubt there were strong representations made to King James of the fitness of the colony for silk raising. Sir Thomas Gates, about the year 1610, was adjured by the Council of Virginia to "deal plainly with them" as to the capabilities of the new country and the prospects of the colony. He replied under " a solemn and sacred oath". In the course of this testimony he says:

There are innumerable white mulberry trees, which in so warme a climate may cherish and feede millions of Silkeworms, and return us in a very short time as great plenty of Silke as is vented into the whole world from all parts of Italy. (*a*)

For some years the colony was in a forlorn condition, (*b*) but in 1619 great efforts were made for its relief. Silk culture appears prominently as among the means to help the people out of their poverty, in the measures taken by legislative and governing powers on both sides of the Atlantic. The colonial assembly, in its first brief session of five days, found time to order the planting of mulberry trees and the rearing of silkworms. (*c*) The following is recorded as one of the items in a sort of invoice described as "A Note of the Shipping, Men and Provisions sent to Virginia by the Treasurer and Company in the Yeere 1619": (*d*)

---

a Purchas, his Pilgrimes, vol. iv, p. 1734.

b Sir Dudley Diggs asserts in 1615: "The great Expence that the nobility and Gentry have been at in planting Virginia is in no way recompensed by the poor Returns from thence." An Historical and Chronological Deduction of the Origin of Commerce, by Adam Anderson; London, folio edition, 1764; vol. i, p 494

c A Reporte of the Manner of Proceedings in the General Assembly, convented at James City in Virginia, July 30, 1619, by John Pory, the Secretary and Speaker.

d Purchas, vol. iv, p. 1777.

Silke: for which that Countrey is exceeding proper, having innvmerable store of Mvlberry Trees of the best, and some Silkwormes naturally found upon them, producing excellent Silke: some whereof is to be seene. For the sitting vp of which Commoditie his Majesty hath beene graciously pleased now the second time (the former having miscarried) to bestow vpon the Company plenty of Silkwormes-seed of his owne store, being the best.

The royal gardens at Oatlands furnished this supply of eggs, and from there also a person skilled in silk culture was sent to give instruction to the colonists. In the same year King James issued his famous "decree and proclamation" against tobacco, checking its import into England by an almost prohibitory duty. Nor was that duty intended to protect home industry in the Virginia weed, for another proclamation in that year forbade the cultivation of tobacco in England and Wales, and the plants growing in the kingdom were uprooted. The king was undoubtedly anxious to have silk raised instead of tobacco throughout his domain.· Another circumstance made 1619 a memorable year; it was then that this most christian monarch, while striving to check the comparatively harmless vice of using tobacco, sanctioned and authorized by royal charter a joint-stock company in London with the exclusive privilege of taking negroes from Africa into slavery in the colonies. The effects of that enterprise were permanent.

Sending out silkworm eggs from England was followed in 1622 by the most peremptory and urgent directions to encourage silk culture. Aid was promised on the one hand to colonists who entered heartily into the work, and on the other hand punishments were ordered for those who neglected the matter. As will be seen by the documents, the king was impatient and would brook no further delay:

His Maiesties gracious Letter to the Earle of South-hampton, Treasurer, and to the Counsell and Company of Virginia here: commanding the present setting vp of Silke Workes, and planting of Vines in Virginia: (*a*)

Right trusty and wellbeloued, We greete you well: whereas We understand, that the soyle in Virginia naturally yieldeth store of excellent Mulberry trees, We have taken into our Princely consideration the great benefit that may grow to the Adventurers and Planters, by the breede of Silkewormes and setting vp of Silkeworkes in those parts. And therefore of Our gracious inclination to a designe of so much honour and advantage to the publik, We have thought good, as at sundry other times, so now more particularly to recommend it to your speciall care, hereby charging and requiring you to take speedy order, that our people there use all possible diligence in breeding Silkewormes, and erecting Silkeworkes, and that they rather bestow their travell in compassing this rich and solid Commodity, then in that of Tobacco; which, beside much vnnecessary expence, brings with it many dis-

---

a Purchas, vol. iv, p. 1787, *et seq.*

orders and inconueniences. And for as much as Our seruant, John Bonoell (a) hath taken paines in setting downe the true vse of the Silkeworme, together with the Art of Silkemaking, and of planting Vines, and that his experience and abilities may much conduce to the aduancement of this businesse; We doe hereby likewise require you to cause his directions, both for the said Silkeworkes and Vineyards, to be carefully put in practice thorowout our Plantations there, that so the worke may goe on cheerefully, and receive no more interruptions nor delayes.

Giuen vnder Our Signet, at Our Pallace of Westminster, the ninth day of Iuly, in the twentieth yeare of our Raigne of England, France and Ireland, and of Scotland the fiue and fiftieth.

To our right trusty and right wellbeloued Cousin and Councellour, HENRY, Earle of South-hampton, Treasurer of our Plantation in Virginia, and to Our trusty and wellbeloued, the Deputy, and others of our said Plantation.

Virginia. WINDEBANK.

The royal instructions were transmitted and strongly enforced, as appears by the following communication:

The Treasurour, Counsell and Company of *Virginia*, to the Gouvernour and Counsell of State in *Virginia* residing:

After our very hearty commendations: His Sacred Majesty, out of his high wisedome and care of the noble Plantation of Virginia, hath beene graciously pleased to direct his Letters to us here in *England*, thereby commanding vs to aduance the setting vp of *Silkworkes*, and planting of *Vineyards;* as by the Copy herewith sent, you may perceive. The intimation of his Maiesties pleasure, we conceiue to be a motiue sufficient, to induce you to imploy all your indeuors to the setting forward those two Staple Commodities of *Silke* and *Wine;* which brought to their perfection, will infinitely redound to the honour, benefit, and comfort of the Colony, and of this whole Kingdome: yet we, in discharge of our duties, doe againe renew our often and iterated Instructions, and inuite you cheerefully, to fall vpon these two so rich, and necessary Commodities. And if you shall finde any person, either through negligence or wilfulnesse, to omit the planting of *Vines*, and *Mulberry trees*, in orderly and husbandly manner, as by the Booke is prescribed, or the placing of conuenient roomes for the breeding of *Wormes;* we desire they may by seuere censures and punishment, be compelled thereunto. And on the contrary, that all fauour and possible assistance be giuen to such as yeelde willing obedience to his *Highnesse* Commands therein. The breech or performance whereof, as we are bound to giue a strict account, so will it also be required of you the *Gouernour* and *Counsell* especially. Herein there can be no Plea, either of difficulty or impossibility; but all the contrary appeares, by the naturall abundance of those two excellent Plants afore-named euerywhere in *Virginia;* neither will such excuses be admitted, nor any other pretences serue, whereby the businesse be at all delayed; and as wee formerly sent at our great charge the *French Vignerons* to you, to teach you their Art; so for the same pvrpose we now commend this Booke vnto you, to serue as an Instructour to euery one, and send you store of them to be dispersed ouer the whole Colony, to euery Master of a Family one, Silke-seede you shall receiue also by this Ship, sufficient to store euery man: so that there wants nothing,

---

a This name is also spelled "Bonoeil". Vid. Barham's Essay, which also gives these letters.

but indvstry in the Planter, svddenly to bring the making of *Silke* to its perfection: which either for their owne benefit (we hope) they will willingly indeuour, or by a wholesome and necessary seuerity they must be inforced.

The letter goes on to state that it is of urgent character, and not to be taken as a common instruction. There is a marginal note stating that the "Booke" referred to contains good rules for silkworks, vines, and other husbandry. The document itself is signed by the Earl of Southampton. In 1623 the legislature of the colony issued further orders requiring mulberry trees to be planted, the fine for neglect being 20 pounds of tobacco. The act also offered a premium of 50 pounds of tobacco for every pound of reeled silk produced. (*a*)

At this point we can give what is probably the earliest quotation for raw silk in this country. It includes also the price of cocoons; here described as "coddes" and elsewhere as "bottomes". Too much stress should not be laid upon the accuracy of the record, as it was put in print nearly thirty years after the period to which it refers. The traffic could not have been large, but there is other evidence that some silk was made, and we may in any case regard the quotations as "offering prices" of that date:

From "A valuation of the commodities growing and to be had in Virginia: valued in the year 1621. And since those Times improved in all more or lesse, in some ⅓, in others ¼, in many double, and in some treble."

"Silk Coddes, two shillings sixpence the pound.

"Raw silk, 13*s*. 4*d*. the pound, now at 25*s*. and 28*s*. per pound.

"Silk grasse to be used for Cordage, 6*d*. the pound." This has reference to a fibrous plant growing wild and extensively in the colony. Queen Elizabeth had a gown made of this material, described as "a substantial and rich piece of Grograine". It was hoped that by cultivation the fibre of this grass could be improved so as to equal the silk which it was said to resemble. (*b*)

The art of weaving broad silks was introduced into England, and those who were so engaged were included in the great company of weavers, at or about this period; the date generally assigned for the event being 1620. The silk throwsters of London formed a corporation and were chartered in 1629. (*c*) The needs of the growing manufacture in the mother country probably caused the advance of price of the raw material in the colony. Royal encouragement was of brief duration. The king and the Virginia Company quar-

---

a This curious act was reproduced in full in a monthly publication, *The American Silk Grower*, Philadelphia, December, 1838.

b Virginia: More especially the South part thereof * * *—the fertile Carolana, by Edward Williams; second edition, London, 1650; reprint, Force's Tracts, vol. iii, No. xi, p. 51.

c Act 5, Charles I. Anderson's Origin of Commerce, ii, pp. 4 and 36.

relled, and the latter were ousted from all their rights and powers by proclamation of James I, July 15, 1624. On his accession to the throne in the next year, Charles I took the government of the colony into his own hands. (*a*) Very little progress in silk culture seems to have been made during the reign of that unfortunate monarch. Under the Protectorate, interest in the subject was revived, and several curious tracts were written on behalf of the industry. The most noted of these essays were by ("E. W.") Edward Williams (*b*) (1650) and Hartlib (1652-'55). Williams regards the production of silk as one of the wonders of nature ; a mystery, which if taught to the savages, might impress them with pious awe. He says: (*c*)

1. First, the Indian is naturally curious and very ingenious, which they show in all their works and imitations; the only thing that frights them from bringing any work to perfection, is the labour attending it.

2. But to feed his curiosity, there is nothing in the world more proper than this curious atome of Nature the Silkeworme: to see this untaught Artist spin out his transparent bowels, labour such a monument out of his owne intralls, as may be the shame, the blush of Artists, such a Robe that Solomon in all his glory might confesse the meannesse of his apparell, in relation to the workemen, cannot but bring them to admiration; and that those spirits whose thoughts are of a higher wing than ordinary, may bee convinced of a divine power of the hand of God in the Creation: which gayned upon him, it will not be impossible to drive him to an acknowledgment of Redemption, if private ends or any other respect than that to God's glory, possesse not those who should cover a multitude of sinnes, by winning a soule to his Creator, and forcing him from the jaws of his Destroyer.

3. In this curiosity there is little or no labour (a thing which they abhorre) their women and children will bee sufficient to goe through with it; and if they could but be brought to it, our Trade with them for Silke would be of greater consequence, then all their Furs or other commodities put together.

This is followed by an estimate that the silk thus produced might be purchased in barter at five shillings per pound; the barter to be for British cloths which it was hoped the Indians might be induced to want when they were so far civilized as to require clothing. A similar idea impressed itself on Samuel Hartlib, who was an enterprising merchant of London, and who has a better chance of remembrance in literature than the other silk essayists of the period, since Milton dedicated to him a Treatise on Education. The title of one of Hartlib's books is itself a curiosity:

"The Reformed Virginian Silk-Worm, or, a Rare and New Discovery of a speedy way, and easie means, found out by a young Lady in *England*, she having

---

a Jefferson's Notes on Virginia, p. 182.

b Virginia's Discovery of Silke-Wormes, with their Benefit. An Implanting of Mulberry Trees, by E. W., London, 1650. The engravings in this work are exquisitely quaint.

c Force's Tracts, vol. iii, No. xi, p. 93.

made full proof thereof in *May, Anno* 1652. For the feeding of Silk-worms in the Woods, on the Mulberry-Tree-leaves in *Virginia:* Who after forty dayes time, present their most rich golden-coloured silken Fleece, to the instant wonderful enriching of all the Planters there, requiring from them neither cost, labour, or hindrance in any of their other employments whatsoever. And also to the good hopes that the *Indians,* seeing and finding that there is neither Art, Skill, or Pains in the thing: they will readily set upon it, being by the benefit thereof inabled to buy of the *English* (in way of Truck for their Silk-bottoms) all those things that they most desire." (*a*)

In his introduction, Mr. Hartlib refers to the efforts of King James to extend silk culture in England by planting mulberry trees and rearing silkworms. The Hartlib essay is addressed to the planters of Virginia, and is designed to urge them in the same industry and to exhibit the superior advantages they may enjoy by obtaining the cocoons of certain native insects producing wild silk. The Indians were to be pressed into this service, in the hope of converting them to christianity and making a profit at the same time, and the essay overflows with pious phrases and calculations of gain, curiously intermingled. The insect and its cocoon are described as of extraordinary size, as follows:

"The fashion of the Botome.(*b*) The Silk Bottome of the naturall Worm in *Virginia,* found there in the woods, is ten Inches about, and six Inches in length to admiration: & whereas ours in Europe have their Sleave and loose Silke on the outside; and then in a more closer covering they intombe themselves. These rare Worms, before they enclose themselves up, fill with silk the great emptiness, and afterward inclose themselves in the middle of it, so they have a double bottom. The loose Sleave silk is all on the outside of that compass, for if that were reckoned in, the compass of the Bottom would far exceed this proportion: But this is sufficient to be the Wonder of the whole world: to the Glory of the Creatour, and Exaltation of VIRGINIA." (*c*)

The essay concludes with "Ryming lines", "collected by a young Scholar, out of Letters", sent from Virginia to England. A few specimens will suffice:

> Where Wormes and Food doe naturally abound,
> A Gallant Silken Trade must there be found:
> Virginia excells the World in both,
> Envie nor malice can gaine say this troth. (*d*)
>
> *   *   *   *
>
> Her Worms are huge whose bottoms dare
> With Lemmons of the largest size compare.
>
> *   *   *   *
>
> Master William Wright of Nansamound
> Found Bottoms above seven Inches round. (*e*)

---

a London, 1655.
b This word is variously spelled.
c Hartlib, p. 18.
d *Ibid.*, p. 33.
e *Ibid.*, p. 34.

But although a governor of the Colony, Edward Diggs, joined the ranks of the essayists, (a) it does not appear that the planters were stirred to much activity in raising silk. The hopes that illumine the pages of many writers of the period were slenderly if at all fulfilled. The causes of such complete failure are not obvious. The historian Bancroft has summed up the subject in a resounding sentence which declares that "the culture of silk, long, earnestly, and frequently commended to the attention of Virginia, is successfully pursued only where a superiority of labor exists in a redundant population".

Punishments and rewards were alike in vain. An act of the colonial assembly in 1656 imposed a fine of ten pounds of tobacco on any planter who had not at least ten mulberry trees to every hundred acres. A premium of 4,000 pounds of tobacco was given as a reward for remaining in the business of silk culture in the colony. In 1657, 10,000 pounds of tobacco were offered to any one exporting £200 worth of raw silk, and 5,000 pounds of tobacco to any one producing 1,000 pounds of "wound silk" in a year. The act of 1656 was repealed in 1658, but was revived in 1660. A reward was offered in 1662, (b) of 50 pounds of tobacco for every pound of silk raised, and Sir William Berkeley, the governor of Virginia, received, September 12, pressing instructions from King Charles II to urge forward the industry. But it is difficult to find any record of the product. There is indeed a tradition, treated rather incredulously by historians, that the king at his coronation in 1660 wore a robe and hose of Virginia silk. A letter of instructions to Governor Berkeley gives color to this legend in the following phrase: "We ourself having made experience of the Silk grown there and finding it to be equal to any we have seen." (c)

In 1666 all acts giving bounties for silk or requiring mulberry trees to be planted were repealed; in 1669 there was a brief revival of the bounties, but after that, all legislative encouragement ceased. (d) The mulberry had been abundantly planted, and one claimant for bounties proved that he had 70,000 trees growing in 1664. Governor Berkeley "made essays" of flax, hemp, silk, and other

---

a Writing in 1654, Governor Diggs mentions that he had raised "400 pound weight of silk bottomes", and he adds: "This next spring there will be divers tryals made of the hopeful natural Worms that you so highly prize, and not without good cause." *Hartlib*, p. 28; also, Barham, p. 100.

b History of Virginia, by Robert Beverley; London, 1705, vol. i, p. 58.

c Hazard's Historical Collections, vol. ii, p. 608.

d Twentieth Congress, 1st sess., H. R. Doc. 158, p. 14.

productions, (*a*) and in 1671, in an answer to the committee on plantations, used the cautious expression: "Of late we have begun to make silk." In that year the number of persons engaged in silk manufacture in England was estimated at 40,000. Perhaps if the pressure brought to bear upon silk culture had been equally applied to the making of silk goods, Virginia might have shared in England's prosperity, and both branches of the industry could have been sustained. But this was no part of the colonial policy of Great Britain. Even the trained skill of Piedmont was not welcomed. Cromwell's navigation laws of 1651 not only prohibited receipt or export by other than English-built ships, manned by Englishmen, but also forbade that any alien should manage a trade or factory in the colonies. (*b*)

The Virginia legislature did indeed make an effort toward manufacture, by ordering each county to establish a loom and support a weaver, but the act was repealed in 1684, and seems to have been of no practical effect. There are no records of any further noteworthy production of silk in Virginia, though we are told that "the mulberry tree grows there like a weed, and silkworms have been observed to thrive extremely and without hazard." (*c*) Virginia's weed supplanted even the thrifty mulberry. Formerly, says the historian of the colony, "there was great encouragement given for making of linen, silk, etc., and all persons not performing several things toward producing of them were put under a fine. Now, all encouragement of such things is taken away or entirely dropped by the assemblies, and such manufactures are always neglected when tobacco brings anything of a price."(*d*) Lastly, about the year 1698, Governor Nicholson sent a memorial to England, in which he urged parliament to pass an act forbidding the plantations to make their own clothing. But there was no necessity for choking the provincial industry; it was dying a natural death.

During the latter part of the seventeenth century, a large body of French Huguenots settled in the southern part of the province of Carolina. (*e*) They brought with them a knowledge of various industries, and are probably to be credited with the earliest production

---
a Beverley's Virginia, i, p. 58.
b Ibid., p. 51.
c Ibid., iii, p. 239.
d Ibid., iii, p. 261.
e The official division of the Carolinas into North and South was not made until 1728, when the province was taken under direct control of the crown. Philos. and Polit. Hist. of the Carolinas, by the Abbé Raynal; Edinburgh Transl., i, p. 210.

of silk-mixed fabrics in this country. "South Carolina hath gained a manufacture of linens by means of the French refugees, and invented a new kind of stuff by mixing the silk it produces with its wool."(a) At about the same period, 1693 to 1702, a vigorous though restricted attempt at silk culture was made by Sir Nathaniel Johnson, and the locality of this undertaking bore the name of Silk Hope for more than a century. (b) The results are thus summarized: "However, Sir Nathaniel Johnson, after all his pains, rather showed what might have been done toward the culture of silk in that province, than made such progress in it as to render the commodity of national advantage." (c) There was no slackening of demand for raw silk in the mother country; the silk-throwing mill of Sir Thomas Lombe was started at Derby, England, in 1719. (d) A writer of that date states the whole case with precision.

Silk is a Commodity of great Use in England for many Manufactures, it being imported to us from *France, Italy, Sicily, Turkey*, and the *East Indies;* and there is no Foreign Commodity, which exhausts more of our Treasure. I am not so vain as to promise, this country can furnish Great-Britain with so much Silk as is therein manufactured, which would amount to above a Million *Sterling* annually: But if this Province is ever settled (it abounding in most Parts with Forests of Mulberry Trees both White and Red) and we keep a good Correspondence with the Natives, which is both our Duty and Interest, certainly a considerable Quantity of Silk may be here produced. It hath been already experimented, in *South Carolina*, by *Sir Nathaniel Johnson* and others, which would have return'd to great Account, but that they wanted Hands, Labourers being not to be hir'd but at vast Charge. Yet if the Natives or *Negroes* were employ'd who delight in such easy light Labours, we could have that done for less than One shilling, which costs them more than six. Now I appeal to all good *Englishmen*, if we can raise only a Tenth part of the Silk expended in *Great Britain*, etc., and perhaps half an Age hence the Fifth, whether it would not be very beneficial to our Native Country?(e)

The foregoing extract seems likely to be of interest to modern promoters of schemes for employing Southern negroes in silk raising, since the suggestion of such service as peculiarly suitable for the colored race is thus antedated more than 150 years. Joshua Gee, an eminent English publicist, made an estimate that the labor of slaves employed in raising silk would produce about twice as much value as in planting sugar or tobacco. (f) Nor is the list of

---

a Raynal, i, p. 213.
b Ramsay's Hist. S. C., ii, p. 475.
c Hist. Acct. S. C. and Ga., by Dr. Alex. Hewatt, i, p. 157.
d 20th Congress, 1st sess., H. R. Doc. 158, p. 13. This document will hereafter be cited simply as the "Rush Letter".
e A Description of the English Province of South Carolina, by Daniel Coxe; London, 1722, p. 90.
f The Trade and Navigation of Great Britain. London; 1738, chap. xxx, p. 146.

possible silk culturists ended when it includes planters, Huguenots, Indians, and negroes. Another writer, who has taken great pains with calculations of profit, urges that the mother country should send her paupers and "small offenders" to South Carolina; "it must be a weak Hand indeed that cannot earn bread where Silkworms and white mulberry trees are so plenty." (*a*) The argument will commend itself to the managers of state charities:

Let us suppose that Twenty Five Thousand of the most helpless People in Great Britain were settled there at an expense of half a Million of Money; the Easiness of the Labour in winding off the Silk and tending the Silk Worm would agree with the most of those who throughout the Kingdom are chargeable to the Parishes. That Labour with the benefit of Land stock'd for them *gratis*, would well subsist them, and save our Parishes near Two Hundred Thousand Pounds a Year directly in their annual payments; not to compute (what) would also be saved indirectly, by the Unwillingness of many pretended Invalids to go the Voyage, who would then betake themselves to industrious Courses to gain a Livelyhood. (*b*)

There was a general belief that England lost money by the sums paid to foreigners for the raw material from which goods were made. This notion appears prominently in writings upon economical subjects throughout the seventeenth and eighteenth centuries. It began with the birth of English textile manufacture, and lasted till the use of the steam engine altered the conditions and problems of industry. Silk had to bear the brunt of this obloquy.

As this Nation very much inclines to the Wearing Silk Garments in imitation of the French, to the great Discouragement of our Woolen Manufacture, the Manufacture of Silk from our Plantations would not only enable us to supply ourselves, but to be capable of Exporting very great Quantities of Silk fully Manufactured. (*c*)

In fact, however, the silk industry of the mother country had made some notable advances. English manufacturers, who had long been dependent upon Italy for thrown silk, were now making their own tram and organzine. The machinery in general use was, indeed, such as is driven by the hand or foot of the operative; but there was one great exception, a power-driven machine in the factory of Sir Thomas Lombe. The importance of this invention seems to have been fairly recognized.

As we have but one Water engine for throwing silk in the Kingdom, if that should be destroyed by Fire or any other Accident, it would make the Continuance of throwing fine Silk among us very precarious; and it is very much to be doubted whether all the Men now living in the Kingdom could make such another.(*d*)

---

a A New and Accurate Account of the Provinces of South Carolina and Georgia; London, 1732, chap. v., p. 55.
b Ibid., chap. iv., p. 51.
c Gee's Trade and Navigation, chap. xxx
d Ibid. "This amazingly grand machine contains 26,586 wheels and 97,746 movements, which work 73,726 yards of organzine silk thread every time the water-wheel goes round, being thrice in one minute. and 318,504,960 yards in one day and night " The buildings occupied by the machinery were an eighth of a mile in length. Anderson, Origin of Commerce, ii, p. 284.

Far more anxiety for silk culture in the colonies was displayed in England than in America. The planters did not take serious interest in the business. A colony of Swiss who settled in South Carolina about 1733-'35 (*a*) under the leadership of John Peter Purry, of Neufchatel, was successful in raising silk and cotton, and was credited with some progress in manufacture. The mulberry tree flourished in the light and sandy soil of the pine lands. (*b*) The excellent quality of South Carolina silk was certified by Sir Thomas Lombe, who considered it equal in strength and beauty to that of Italy. (*c*) But as to amount produced, the following figures speak for themselves:

Raw silk exported from North and South Carolina to Great Britain between 1731 *and* 1755 (*d*)

	Pounds.
1731 to 1741	
1742	181½
1743-1747	
1748 (8 boxes)	52
1749	46
1750	118
1751 and 1752	
1753	11
1754	
1755	5½
Total in twenty-five years	251

In the last named year Mrs. Pinckney, who is also famous as the introducer of the indigo plant into South Carolina, took with her to England some silk which she had raised and spun near Charleston; three complete dresses were made therefrom; one was presented to the princess dowager of Wales, one to Lord Chesterfield, and one remained an elegant heirloom in possession of the family for more than fifty years. (*e*) (During the Revolutionary War the Pinckneys won renown which outshone that of the arts of peace.) It is said that 630 pounds of silk were raised in 1765 at Silk Hope plantation. Perhaps South Carolina did not get full credit for her silk product, as much of it went to Georgia to be reeled, resulting

---

a Raynal, vol. i, p. 223.
b Description of the Province of South Carolina, by George Milligen, London, 1770, p, 8.
c Letter of Thomas Lombe to the Trustees of Georgia, January 31. 1732.
d A Description of South Carolina, London, 1761, p. 96 (authorship somewhat uncertainly ascribed to Governor Glenn, of that province).
e Ramsay, I, p. 221.

in its ultimate shipment from Savannah. There is some curious evidence of popular belief or rumor to this effect, which will be mentioned hereafter. Charleston people wanted a filature in their city to prevent the diversion of trade, and an act was passed to meet the wish, in 1766, by the colonial assembly. This was followed by a grant of £1,000 to support the enterprise. Meanwhile the London Society of Arts was giving handsome bounties for cocoons and raw silk, and kept up the offer till 1772; Parliament in 1769 granted a bounty of 25 per cent. for seven years on all raw silk imported from the colonies. (*a*) But the Revolutionary War put a stop to the bounties and the silk industry of South Carolina ceased to exist. The Abbé Raynal has pronounced its funeral oration. That philosophical writer of course offers a theory; silk was not exported because negresses were not imported. He concludes:

Yet the progress of this branch of trade has not been answerable to so promising a beginning. The blame has been laid on the inhabitants of the colony, who, buying only negro men from whom they receive an immediate and certain profit, neglected to have women who, with their children, might have been employed in bringing up silkworms, an occupation suitable to the weakness of that sex and to the tenderest age.(*b*)

Tracing the silk industry in the order of its starting at different points in this country, we find it introduced into Louisiana next after South Carolina. In 1716 the notorious John Law formed, at Paris, the Mississippi Company, which was a leading feature in a series of speculative schemes that were afterward called the great South Sea bubble. Louisiana had been settled by the French. The city of New Orleans was founded in 1718, and about that time the whole colony was transferred to the Mississippi Company by a grant of the French crown. Law organized and sent out a large expedition in 1718. In the glittering prospectus (*c*) of this speculation, one of the items was the culture of silk on the banks of the Mississippi, and this part of the programme was in a measure carried out.

---

a Raynal, ii, p. 160.

b Ibid., ii, p. 159.

c Anderson gives a long abstract of the projects of the South Sea Company. Under one section there are the following details.

"For the *Silk* and *Cotton* manufactures, viz:

1. For the raising of *Silk-worms*.

2. Another for the planting of *Mulberry Trees* and breeding of *Silk-worms* in *Chelsea Park* where 2,000 of those trees were actually planted and many large and expensive edifices were erected; the remains whereof are now (1764) scarcely to be seen. (Particulars about these trees and their estimated value as assets of a stock company can be found in *Barham's Essay*, pp. 9?, 105, and 278. It was expected that they would produce 14,000 pounds of silk, worth £14,000, per year.)

3. For making of *Muslin*.

4. For improving the Cotton and the Silk and Cotton Manufactures.

5. Another for improving the Silk Manufactures." Origin of Commerce, ii, p. 293.

Many mulberry trees were planted in and near **New Orleans.** Failure to reach profitable results seems, however, to have overtaken every branch of Law's schemes. "The Ancient India Company never sent more than a few ship loads of its products to France, and the unfortunate Mississippi colony furnished next to nothing." (*a*) After the South Sea bubble burst, the ownership of the land and the control of the colony reverted to the crown. The French held possession till 1762, when they ceded it to Spain. We do not read of any considerable silk product Favorable soil and climate, and a knowledge of the business on the part of the colonists, were not wanting; but legislative bounties were.

Georgia, which had been part of the "fertile Carolinas," was made by royal charter a separate province, in 1732, and placed in control of a board of trustees. This event became the occasion of an urgent pressure in favor of silk culture. The trustees themselves heartily favored the project, and fixed upon silk and wine as the leading staples to be raised for export, (*b*) silk being chief in their esteem.(*c*) Sir Thomas Lombe wrote a forcible letter on the subject to the trustees, declaring that silk culture "appears to me as beneficial to the kingdom, attended with as little hazard or difficulty, as much wanted, and which may as soon be brought to perfection in a proper climate, as any undertaking so considerable in itself that I ever heard of." (*d*) The trustees at their meeting in June, 1732, adopted a rule requiring settlers to plant a certain proportion of mulberry trees. In their respective grants ten years were allowed for the cultivation of the soil, and 100 white mulberry trees were to be planted on every ten acres when cleared. Power was vested in the trustees to enter upon lands that remained uncultivated.(*e*) A colonial seal was ordered, containing on one side a representation of silkworms, some beginning and others having finished their webs, with the motto: *Non sibi sed aliis.* This, says one historian, was "a very proper emblem, signifying that neither the first trustees nor their successors could have any views to their own interest." (*f*) It does not seem to have been meant, by the use of this motto, to suggest that

---

a The Eighteenth Century, by Paul Lecroix; London, 1876, p. 222.

b Judge Law's Oration, Georgia Historical Society Collections, i, p. 26.

c An Impartial Inquiry into the State and Utility of the Province of Georgia, by Benj. Martin, secretary of the trustees of the colony; London, 1741, reprint Ga. Hist. Soc., i, p. 160.

d Appendix, Ga. Hist. Soc. Collns., ii, p. 311.

e History of Georgia, by Thomas McCall, i, p. 21.

f Hewatt's Hist. S. C. and Ga., ii, p. 18. McCall's History, i, p. 25.

the colonists, in raising silk for British manufacturers, were laboring not for themselves but for others.

Late in 1732 a man from Piedmont was sent out by the trustees to teach the colonists the art of reeling. Several public writers urged the enterprise on various grounds of economy and profit. An estimate in 1733 (based on the assumption that the yearly import of raw silk by Great Britain from Piedmont amounted to £300,000 in value) set forth that the successful raising of silk in Georgia would save the mother country £100,000 per annum. (*a*) Another estimate in the same year made the annual import by Great Britain of thrown silk alone—excluding raw silk—300,000 pounds, equal to £300,000 in value.(*b*) It was therefore an occasion of much congratulation in 1734-'35 when General Oglethorpe took with him to England eight pounds of colonial silk, and showed it to the trustees, who presented it to Queen Caroline. Under royal instructions Sir Thomas Lombe took charge of the precious consignment, and had it thrown and woven at his factory; so that in 1735, upon the king's birthday, the queen honored the colony by appearing at a levee in a dress said to be entirely made of Georgia silk.(*c*) But even this neat little episode has suffered by the breath of detraction. A certain Dr. Patrick Tailfer and others, who perhaps bore no good will to General Oglethorpe, have stated in a spiteful way, that most, if not all of this silk, was raised in South Carolina.(*d*)

In 1735 a plot of ground was laid out at one end of the town of Savannah, and was planted with vines and mulberry trees at public expense. The "trustees' garden", as the plot was termed, proved to have been ill-located, the soil being sandy and arid; though on this and similar points authorities vary. It is certain that the trustees requested the selection of some other spot of ground, but their wishes were not fulfilled.(*e*) The site was on the bank of the river within view of the ocean. Plants and trees, native and foreign, in great variety, including the fig, orange, pomegranate, olive, coffee, cocoa, and cotton, were set out; but chief attention was given to the mulberry. Every planter wanting mulberry trees was supplied with them,

---

a A New and Accurate Account of the Provinces of So. Ca. and Ga.; chap. v, pp. 58, 60.

b Reasons for Establishing the Colony of Georgia; London, 1733, reprint Ga. Hist. Soc., i, p. 208.

c The Dead Towns of Georgia, by Charles C. Jones; Savannah, 1878, p. 26.

d A True and Historical Narrative of the Colony of Georgia; Charleston, 1741, reprint Ga. Hist. Soc., ii, p. 205.

e McCall, i, pp. 55, 57.

gratis, from this nursery. The promise to supply these trees was a feature and condition of the land-grants to colonists.(*a*) One writer describing the garden in glowing terms of praise, declares the soil excellent and the situation "delightful."(*b*) Others hold a totally opposite opinion and say that the place was "one of the most barren spots of land in the colony, being only a hill of dry sand; great sums of money were thrown away upon it from year to year to no purpose."(*c*)

Several Italians of both sexes were brought in 1736 at the trustees' expense from Piedmont in charge of a Mr. Amatis. The foreigners were proficient in the arts of silk culture and reeling; the men were ordered to teach male English colonists to raise mulberry trees, the women to take English girls as apprentices in rearing worms and reeling from cocoons.(*d*) "In Italy and in the south of France, young girls carry the eggs in their bosom, and hatch them by their natural heat. In other countries this is done by means of manure or hot-houses."(*e*) It is not specified which of these processes was taught to the English girls. Some of the Italians behaved badly; one of them stole the reels, broke the copper pans,(*f*) spoiled all the eggs he could not steal, and fled to South Carolina; but a little seed and a few faithful Piedmontese were left.(*g*)

Meanwhile a number of **Protestants**, driven out of their home in the valley of the Salza, Bavaria, had emigrated to Georgia and founded a town, which they called Ebenezer, about 25 miles above Savannah, near to, but not quite on the river.(*h*) They brought with them several useful arts, and soon accomplished more in the business of raising silk, with far less fuss, than their neighbors at Savannah. They co-operated with the trustees, and before long had two reels

---

a McCall, i, p. 63.

b A Voyage to Georgia, by Francis Moore; London, 1744, pp. 29, 30.

c A True and Historical Narrative; reprint Ga. Hist. Soc., ii, p. 205.

d A Voyage to Georgia, p. 31.

e Treatise on Rearing Silk Worms, by Count Von Hazzi, of Munich; Transl. U. S. 20th Cong., 1st Sess., H. R. Doc. 226; sec. 61, p. 77. There are precise instructions on this point in Noel Chomel's Dictionaire Œconomique (2 vol. fol., Paris, 1718) as follows: "In order to hatch the eggs at their proper time, the women must keep them in their bosoms and the men in their pockets, and on nights between warm pillows put under your bolster or bed, and thus to continue for three days without looking upon them, for fear lest the cold air injure them." Barham's Essay, p. 118.

f The pans were used for baking the cocoons, to kill the chrysalides.

g A Voyage to Georgia, p. 31.

h Raynal, i, p. 223. McCall, i, p. 49. The Long Island Historical Society of Brooklyn, N. Y., possesses very complete records of this emigration and settlement

busy. There are notices at this period of a scheme for interesting the Chickasaw Indians in the work of silk culture.(*a*) English writers were again urging the need of the mother country, and the annual expenditure for silk from Piedmont was estimated at £500,000.(*b*) Even the muse was invoked to stir the lagging colonists, and a poem on the return of General Oglethorpe to Georgia in 1736, winds up—

> Nor less the care
> Of thy young province to oblige the fair;
> Here tend the silkworm in the verdant shade
> The frugal matron and the blooming maid.(*c*)

But as to the export of raw silk, it was admitted in 1740 that "no great entries have been seen of any yet in the custom-house;"(*d*) statements verified by oath declare that "the quantity of silk hitherto made has not been great;"(*e*) the small portion exported "was produced by an Italian family settled in Savannah."(*f*) Another informant sums up the situation with the remark, "there are not as many mulberry trees in the whole province as many a one of the Carolina planters have, nor so much silk as many a one of them makes."(*g*) In fact, the colony of Georgia was at this time in a very weak and impoverished condition, and scarcely able to produce enough of the necessaries of life for its own sustenance. Despite the poverty of the province, the trustees firmly adhered to the line of policy they had marked out: wine and silk were to be cultivated in preference to all other staples.(*h*) "The tracts of land which had been planted with mulberry trees scarcely retained the vestiges of cultivation" in 1744, but new bounties were offered for silk; a filature was built at Savannah, and the implements for reeling were ordered to be furnished.(*i*) The premiums were afterward fixed at two shillings per pound for first quality of cocoons, one shilling for second, and eight pence for third.(*j*) Bounties were also offered in 1749 for proficiency in the art of reeling, and the trustees supplied

---

a Letter to the Trustees; Ga. Hist. Soc. Collns., i, p. 193.
b Life of Oglethorpe, by Thomas Spalding; Ga. Hist. Soc. Collns., i, p. 259.
c A True and Historical Narrative, Preface; reprint, *ibid.*, ii, p. 175. See also Lines addressed to Oglethorpe, *ibid.*, ii, pp. 64, 66.
d An Impartial Inquiry, etc., reprint *ibid.*, i, p. 160.
e A State of the Province of Georgia, Attested upon Oath; London, 1742; reprint, *ibid.*, ii, p. 71.
f An Impartial Inquiry, etc.; reprint *ibid.*, i, p. 192.
g A True and Historical Narrative; reprint, *ibid.*, ii, p. 265
h McCall, i, p. 199.
i Ibid., i, p. 203.
j Ibid., i, p. 238.

the requisite apparatus to competitors. In the following year fourteen young women claimed the bounty and were given permanent employment at the filature, which by this time had an outfit of tools and implements. Special commissioners were sent to the province by the trustees, charged with the duty of promoting the industry.

We are now approaching the period when silk culture in the colonies attained its highest development. An exaggerated notion of the results has been formed by several of the writers who have recorded them. This is chiefly due to neglect in discriminating between cocoons and raw silk. The records from 1757 to 1768, are mostly of the production of cocoons; and of these articles, when fresh or not specially dried, ten or twelve to fourteen pounds are required to furnish one pound of reeled or raw silk (*a*.) The following statements of Georgia production are believed to be authentic :

Years.	Product or Export.
1750	5,300 pounds cocoons received at filature.
1750 to 1754, inclusive	Value of raw silk exported, $8,800.
1756	Amount of raw silk exported, 268 pounds.
1757	1,052 pounds cocoons received at filature.
1758	7,040 pounds cocoons received at filature.
1759	Considerably over 10,000 pounds cocoons received at Savannah.
1764	15,200 pounds cocoons produced.
1766	20,000 pounds cocoons produced.
1768	1,084 pounds raw silk sent to England.
1758 to 1768, inclusive	Nearly 100,000 pounds cocoons received at filature.
1770	291 pounds raw silk produced at Ebenezer; none elsewhere.
1771 (*b*)	438 pounds raw silk produced at Ebenezer; shipped to England.
1772	485 pounds raw silk produced at Ebenezer; shipped to England.
1755 to 1772, inclusive	Amount of raw silk exported, 8,829 pounds.

A careful examination of the foregoing figures will show that they do not involve any contradiction in themselves. They indicate a varying product which culminated in 1766, furnishing from 1750 to 1772 an export averaging 500 pounds of raw silk per annum, and rarely exceeding 1,000 pounds in a single year. It remains to be explained why an assertion has so frequently found place and comment in histories and essays, that in the year 1759, 10,000 pounds of raw silk were exported from Georgia to England. The discrepancy be-

a *E. g.*, the *Bulletin des Soies et des Soieries*, speaking of a recent crop of Upper Italy. says: "34 millions de kilog. de cocons représentant environ 2,400,000 kil. de soie."

b Operations at the filature were discontinued in 1771, and the basins and reels which had been in use there, were distributed among the colonists of Ebenezer.

tween this statement and that of the total export from 1755 to 1772 (which was furnished by the collector of customs at Savannah); has been noticed by some of the more careful writers; others have ignored it; none have traced the error to its origin. It arose in an ambiguous, not to say erroneous, publication from Charleston, South Carolina, which Adam Anderson has fortunately quoted in full. He says:(*a*)

We had public Advices, in this year 1759 from *Charles-Town* in *South Carolina*, of a very hopeful Prospect in that Province of the gradual and considerable Progress and Increase of the Production of *Raw-Silk* there and in the adjoining Province of *Georgia*, *viz:* "In the year 1757, 1,052 Pound weight of *Raw-Silk Balls* were received at the *Filature* in *Georgia:* and the next Year produced no less than 7,040 Pound Weight thereof. And that in this year 1759, there has been received at *Savannah*, the Capital of *Georgia*, considerably above 10,000 Pound Weight of *Raw-Silk*, although the Season has not been favourable. This great Increase of that rich, new, and valuable Production in these Provinces is owing to the increased Number of Hands in raising the same."

It will be seen that the foregoing treats of production, not of export; and therefore presumptively of cocoons, not of reeled silk. At all events the facts were so understood by the Rev. Jared Eliot, of Killingworth, Connecticut (grandson of John Eliot, the "apostle of the North American Indians"), writing in the very year when the advices were received. His version is as follows :

By a late account from *Georgia* it appears that the Silk Manufactory is in a flourishing way. In the year 1757, the Weight of Silk Balls received at the Filature was only 1,052, last Year produced 7,040, and this Year already above 10,000, and it is very remarkable that the Raw Silk, exported from *Georgia* sells at *London* from two to three shillings a Pound more, than that from any other Part of the World. (*b*).

This seems quite correct, except in calling the business a "silk manufactory." On the other hand, the complete error appears in, and has no doubt been mostly propagated among later writers through, the account given in 1816 by Major McCall, which turns the cocoons into raw silk and the production into export, as follows:

In the year 1757, one thousand and fifty pounds of raw silk were received at the filature in Savannah. In 1758, the silk-house was consumed by fire, with a quantity of silk and seven thousand and forty pounds of cocoons or silk balls. In 1759 the colony exported upward of ten thousand weight of raw silk, which sold two or three shillings per pound higher in London, than that of any other country. (*c*)

Great as was the mistake which ascribed to one year as large an

---

a Origin of Commerce; fol. ed., ii, p. 413.

b Essays upon Field Husbandry in New England; Boston, reprint, 1760, note to sixth essay, p. 154. The sixth essay was first published in 1759, printed at New London and New York.

c History of Georgia, i. p. 251.

export as was reached in twenty, it was surpassed in error by a subsequent writer, who says:

> In 1776 more than twenty thousand pounds of raw silk were imported into England from Georgia. (a)

This statement was probably based on the production of 1766, and though brief, had the misfortune to be incorrect in every particular.

The policy of raising silk by means of bounties was pushed to its extreme in 1751, when the trustees of Georgia established the following scale of premiums, which has certainly never been surpassed:

For first quality cocoons, 2s. per pound; if delivered at filature, 3s. 6d.

For second quality cocoons, 1s. 3d. per pound; if delivered at filature, 1s. 8d.

For third quality cocoons, 6d. per pound; if delivered at filature, 1s. 1d.

This was at least two or three times what the cocoons were worth, and is "truly astonishing." (b) The patent of the trustees expired in 1752, and with it all the chartered privileges of the colony, which then became a royal province directly dependent upon the crown for government. (c) Acts of parliament of almost equal liberality soon replaced the measures of the trustees for spurring the silk industry. These acts were various, and the encouragement they gave was fluctuating. One of them, in 1749, admitted raw silk from the American plantations free of duty, and provided that Georgia and South Carolina should thereafter "have the honor of being denominated *Silk Colonies.*" (d) In the same vein of sweetness, George II, June 21, 1754, directed a silver seal to be made for Georgia, bearing on one side a figure representing the genius of the colony offering a skein of silk to the king, with the motto: *Hinc laudem sperate coloni.* (e) For a while the parliamentary bounties were three shillings per pound; in 1766 they were reduced one-half; in 1769 they

---

    a Manual on the Mulberry Tree and Silk Culture, by Jonathan H. Cobb, 4th ed. enlarged; Boston, 1839, app., p. 128. One step in this second series of errors appears in the report of the Committee on Agriculture, United States House of Representatives, May 2, 1826, which says: "In 1766 more than 20,000 pounds of cocoons were exported from thence to England."

    b History of Georgia, by Rev. Wm. Bacon Stevens, M. D.; New York, 1847, vol. i, p. 275.

    c Discourse on Georgia, same author; Boston, 1841, reprint Ga. Hist. Soc., ii, p. 25.

    d Anderson, Origin of Commerce, fol. ed., ii, p. 392.

    e Stevens, Hist. Ga., i, p. 383.

were applied to raw silk exported, giving £25 to every £100 in value. The last-named rate was to continue for seven years, when it was to be reduced to 20 per cent., and again for seven years more at 15 per cent., (*a*) the political occurrences of 1776 being evidently not anticipated.

The silk product rose while the bounties for delivery at Savannah were most liberal, but sank with marvelous rapidity shortly after their reduction, falling to 290 pounds in 1770. Throughout the entire period of silk culture in Georgia the Saltzburghers of Ebenezer were among the largest producers, and were almost the only ones in the years immediately preceding the war of the Revolution who prepared raw silk for export. During the war the French settlers at New Bordeaux, 70 miles above Augusta, are said to have supplied "much of the high country" with sewing-silk made from cocoons of their own raising. (*b*) The industry ceased, however, to attract attention; the last parcel of raw silk offered for sale in Georgia during the century being in the year 1790, when over two hundred-weight was purchased for export at prices ranging from 18 to 26 shillings per pound. (*c*)

Pennsylvania was blest with silk culture at an early date in her history. It was recommended by James Logan to the Penn family in 1725, as "extremely beneficial and promising;" the next year he mentioned that silk from the colony had been sent to England; he "is glad it proves so good." (*d*) A bill had been introduced in 1719 into parliament to restrain the increase of woolen and other manufactures in the colonies. (*e*) A more definite application of the *non sibi sed aliis* principle was urged a few years later, based on a complaint that the colonists were engaged in textile manufacturing, especially in the provinces north of Virginia. The British board of commissioners on trade and plantations made an elaborate report on this subject to parliament in 1732. They say:

It were to be wished that some Expedient might be fallen upon to divert their thoughts from Undertakings of this Nature: So much the rather, because those Manufactures in Process of Time may be carried on in a greater Degree, unless an early Stop be put to their Progress, by employing them in *Naval Stores*.(*f*)

---

a Raynal, ii, p. 106.

b Letter of Thomas McCall to the Secretary of the Treasury in answer to a circular of inquiry sent out in 1826.

c Letter of Charles Harris to the Secretary of the Treasury, in answer as above.

d Annals of Philadelphia, by John F. Watson; Philadelphia, 1830, p. 618.

e Anderson's Origin of Commerce, ii, p. 283.

f *Ibid.*, ii, p. 343.

The conclusion arrived at is as follows :

We would humbly beg Leave to report and submit to the Wisdom of this honourable House, the Substance of what we formerly proposed in our *Report* on the *Silk, Linen* and *Woollen* Manufactures hereinbefore recited; namely, whether it might not be deemed expedient to give those Colonies proper Encouragements for turning their Industry to such Manufactures and Products as might be of Service to Great Britain, and more particularl to the Production of all kinds of *Naval Stores*. (a)

Ultimately it seems to have been considered that the encouragement of silk culture was one of the "expedients" for preventing manufacture. The commissioners addressed a letter in 1734 to the deputy governor of Pennsylvania, Patrick Gordon, asking him what encouragement should be given in order to "engage the colonists to apply their industry to the cultivation of naval stores of all kinds, and likewise of such other products as may be proper for the soil of the said colonies, *and do not interfere with the trade or produce of Great Britain.*" (b) To this Governor Gordon replies that it was the whole study of the merchants how to make returns for the large importations of British manufactures. He recommends among other things that the culture of silk be encouraged, and mentions that small quantities had already been produced in the colony, equal to the best European. (c)

A London paper of February 7, 1765, states that within four days one hundred journeymen silk-throwsters had engaged passage to New York and Philadelphia, under extraordinary encouragements, intending at both places to establish the manufacture of silk. (d) Perhaps the "encouragements" arose partly out of reports concerning efforts which were begun about this time by Dr. Benjamin Franklin. Several hundred pounds sterling were paid to American colonists between 1755 and 1772, for premiums on silk and mulberry trees, by the London Society for the Encouragement of Arts, Manufactures, and Commerce. A pamphlet published by the society mentions that in 1761 the following corresponding members were authorized to pay premiums in their respective colonies : Dr. Jared Eliot, the Rev. T Clap (president of Yale College), and Jared Ingersoll, of Connecticut ; Benjamin Franklin, LL. D., and John Hughes, of Pennsylvania ; George Pollock, Cullen Pollock, and John Rutherford, of North Carolina ; M. Ortoleng: (superintendent of the filature

---

a Anderson's Origin of Commerce. ii, p. 345.

b Archives of Pennsylvania, year 1734, p. 434.

c Hazard's Register of Pennsylvania, i, p. 444.

d History of American Manufactures, by Dr. J. L. Bishop; Philadelphia, 1864, i, p. 362.

at Savannah), of Georgia. The bounties paid in other colonies by the society were probably the same as those announced at that date for Georgia, viz., for first quality of cocoons, 3*d.* per pound; for second quality, 2*d.*, and for third quality, 1*d.* per pound. (*a*) About the year 1766, Dr. Nathaniel Aspinwall, of Mansfield, Connecticut, who had a nursery of white mulberry trees on Long Island, and who was a person of large public spirit and enthusiasm in respect to silk culture, gave a number of such trees to be planted near Philadelphia. (*b*) An act giving bounty for planting the tree had been recently passed by the legislature of New Jersey, and considerable interest was manifested in the subject by other neighboring colonies. The American Philosophical Society of Philadelphia, of which Dr. Franklin was a leading member, gave much consideration to plans for silk culture in 1768 and 1769. Early in 1770 Dr. Franklin, who was then in London, wrote a letter to the society urging these projects and enclosing his correspondence with Dr. Cadwallader Evans, of Philadelphia, upon the subject. (*c*) This seems to have determined the society's course; they took prompt steps for establishing a filature. A subscription for the purpose was started, and during the first year the sum of £875 14*s.* was obtained. Measures were taken to procure supplies of mulberry trees and silkworm eggs, and Dr. Franklin, who was always ready to contribute good advice, sent a copy of a useful work by the Abbé Sauvage. (*d*) An application was made to the assembly to authorize "a public filature," the managers to have power to grant premiums equal to about £500 per annum for five years. The filature was actually opened in June, 1770. (*e*) It was situated in Seventh street, between Arch and High streets. About 2,300 pounds of cocoons were brought thither in

---

a Treatise on the Mulberry and Silkworm, by John Clarke; Philadelphia, 1839, note to p. 111. The Society's premiums for planting mulberry trees were very liberal, vid. Tracts on Practical Agriculture and Gardening, by R. Weston; London, 1773, pp. 31 to 34.

b Historical Collections of Connecticut, by Dr. J. W. Barber; New Haven, 1837, p. 550.

c Watson's Annals, p. 618.

d Mémoires sur l'Education des Vers à Soie, by l'Abbé Boissière de Sauvage; Nismes, 1763, 2 vols., 8 vo. A summary of this treatise was afterward, 1792(?) published by Mr. Odell, of Burlington, New Jersey (Cobb's Silk Manual, p. 85). The Boissière family are still engaged in silk culture in France. Also, Mr. E. V. Boissière is now, and for some years past has been, carrying on this business in connection with his silk factory at Williamsburgh, Franklin county, Kansas.

e J. d'Homergue says the filature was established in 1769, but is probably in error.

1771; of this amount, 1,754 pounds were bought by the managers; two thirds of the cocoons had been raised in New Jersey. (*a*) There is room for doubt as to the disposal of the products. It is more than hinted that all the silk made was absorbed in garments for members of the society. (*b*) J. d'Homergue, who was a competent witness, though perhaps not wholly disinterested, says :

> I have not heard of any raw silk having been prepared at this filature, or sold out of it, yet I have been told that a lady of this city (Philadelphia) had a *negligee* dress manufactured in England out of silk of her own raising. (*c*)

A considerable number of successful attempts at silk culture were made at this time in Pennsylvania, several of which have passed into history. Susannah Wright of Columbia, Lancaster county, a Quaker lady of some literary celebrity, reeled and wove from home grown cocoons a piece of mantua 60 yards in length. A dress was made from this fabric for Queen Charlotte, and for a second time the wife of a British sovereign honored the colonies by appearing at court in American silk. It is further recorded that Susannah Wright had 1,500 worms in 1772, "and could have raised large quantities if encouraged;" (*d*) she also made sewing-silk. Another Quaker lady, Grace Fisher, who was a noted preacher, made some silk fabrics which were presented by Governor Dickinson to Mrs. Catharine Macaulay, the historian. There are several instances about this time of Pennsylvania ladies raising the material for their own clothing, and at least one of a bride thus providing her own wedding garment; but, it is significantly added, "the best dresses worn with us were woven in England." (*e*)

This was the era of the dawn of independence. Many writers have lamented the complete interruption which the Revolutionary War caused to the silk enterprises. In fact, however, the war made the real industry practicable. Silk culture here, to supply manufacturers abroad, was precisely the reverse of a profitable arrangement for this country. "If when we plough, sow, reap, gather, and thresh, we find that we plough, sow, reap, gather, and thresh for others, why should we repeat the unprofitable toil?"(*f*) Legislation to stop manufacturing in America was now the order of the day in

---

a Watson's Annals, p. 618.
b Clarke's Mulberry and Silkworm, p. 115.
c *Ibid.*, note at foot of page. J. d'Homergue was a silk-culturist from Nismes.
d Watson's Annals, p. 619.   *e* *Ibid.*
f Letters from a Farmer in Pennsylvania, by Mr. Dickinson; Boston, 1768; London reprint, 1774; Letter xii, p. 130.

England. An act of Parliament, 3 Geo. II, c. 29, sec. 9, passed in 1750, provided that—

From and after the 24th day of June, 1750, no Mill or other Engine for slitting or rolling of bar Iron, or any plaiting Forge to work with a Tilt-hammer, or any furnace for making of Steel shall be erected or after erection continued in any of His Majesty's colonies in America. (a)

Act. 14 Geo. III, c. 71, was passed in 1774, "To prevent the exportation to foreign parts of utensils made use of in the cotton, linen, woollen, and silk manufactures of this kingdom." The statute imposed a fine of £200 for transgression; such machinery could be seized and confiscated, its holder anywhere was liable to arrest, and even the ship that carried it and the owners of the vessel were reached by the stringent penalties of that law. (b) The United Society for Promoting American Manufactures (Philadelphia) recommended in 1776 an appropriation of £40 for the encouragement of John Marshall, who had constructed some novel machinery for throwing and twisting silk. (c) The invention was at once too early and too late. The arts of peace were suspended, and the people were preparing for war.

Legislation concerning silk culture in Connecticut in 1732 indicated that the industry had made some progress there, even at that early date. The first coat and stockings made of New England silk were worn by Governor Law in 1747; the first silk dress by his daughter; in 1750. (d) Dr. Ezra Stiles, president of Yale college, began a long series of experiments in 1758 by planting three mulberry trees. His carefully kept record of the growth, treatment, and product of the silkworms fills a quarto volume of manuscript still preserved by the college. A professor's gown was made from the fruits of his industry. The experiments were continued till 1790, and during this period Dr. Stiles liberally distributed seeds, eggs, and advice. Nathaniel Aspinwall, who, as has already been mentioned, had a nursery of mulberry trees on Long Island, began about the year 1760 to introduce silk culture into Windham county and other localities in Connecticut. He was successful in planting mulberry orchards at New Haven and Mansfield, (e) and laid the foundation in the latter town of an industry that lasted three-fourths of a century, and paved the way for the present silk manufacture of

---

a Letters from a Farmer, p. 43.
b Force's American Archives; 4th series, vol. i, p. 222.
c Bishop, Hist. Mfrs., i, p. 579.
d Ibid., i. p. 360.
e Memorial of Sundry Inhabitants of the counties of Windham and Tolland; 20th Congress, 1st sess., H. R. Doc. 159, p. 4.

this country. Half an ounce of mulberry seed was sent in 1766 to every parish in Connecticut. (*a*) Several dresses were made from the resulting silk shortly before the Revolution; the town of Mansfield taking the lead in raising the raw material. William Hanks of that town, a large producer, in company with others, projected a silk factory; it is said that one was already built at Lebanon. The outbreak of war checked these undertakings.

There are brief records of silk enterprises in other northern colonies prior to 1776, but they are generally unimportant. The most promising was an attempt of William Molineaux to employ the poor of Boston in spinning, dyeing, and manufacturing silk. He claimed that he had expended £1,200 to £1,500, chiefly for machinery; and he undertook to buy and to manufacture all the silk raised in the province. (*b*) The authorities gave him in 1770 the use of a factory, rent free, to carry out his purpose. It is probable that he undertook to make sewing-silk only, the experiments in weaving at this factory being confined to linen, cotton, and worsted.

Silk history in this country is almost a blank during the struggle for independence, and for several years afterward its records are very faint.

The great demand and high price of breadstuffs, owing to the wars growing out of the French revolution, rendered the cultivation of grain so profitable for many years that the mulberry was neglected. (*c*)

Subsequent revivals of interest in culture and manufacture seemed unimportant at the outset. But small as were these beginnings, they proved more permanent (because they obtained a home market) than all the carefully nursed silk culture for export which had been attempted since the country was settled. The manufacture of sewing-silk gave new life to an industry that had sickened and died when fed on royal favor and parliamentary bounty.

It may here be mentioned, however, that at the period of the Revolution, and for at least fifty years afterward, the making of sewing-silk in this country was chiefly a household art rather than an organized business carried on in a mill or factory. This was the bridge between the silk culture of the colonies and the full-fledged manufacture of the present century: a bridge of essential service, though a chasm yawned at its farther end where many fortunes were engulfed. Connecticut became the chief seat of this new industry,

---

a Barber, Hist. Coll. Conn., p. 550.

b Bishop, i, pp. 362, 376.

c Report of the Committee on Agriculture to the U. S. House of Reps., May 2, 1826. Mass. Agric. Repository and Journal, Vol. ix, No. 2; Boston, 1826.

beginning with an act of the assembly of that state in 1783, to take effect March 1, 1784. (*a*) The passage of the act was chiefly due to the urgent representations of Dr. Stiles and Mr. Aspinwall. The premiums thereby authorized were ten shillings per hundred for planting mulberry trees and preserving them in thrifty condition till three years old; and three pence per pound for producing "raw silk", which was, perhaps, meant to apply to cocoons. In a few years the bounty for planting trees served its purpose throughout the state, and was then discontinued, but the premiums for silk were kept up during a considerable period. In 1789, 200 pounds of silk were raised at Mansfield; in 1793, 362 pounds. (*b*) The quantity steadily increased, and the value of sewing and raw silk made in the counties of New London, Windham, and Tolland, in 1810, aside from consumption of refuse silk in domestic garments, was estimated by Tench Coxe at $28,503. Careful inquiries in the year 1825 showed that the silk product of Windham county was then double that of 1810. (*c*) The Hon. Zalmon Storrs, of Mansfield, replied to the circular of inquiry of July, 1826, that—

Three-fourths of the families in Mansfield are engaged in raising silk, and make, annually, from 5 to 10, 20, and 50 pounds in a family, and one or two have made, each, 100 pounds in a season. It is believed there are annually made in Mansfield and its vicinity from three to four tons.

The last statement was replaced by the more definite figures of 7,000 pounds in 1827. (*d*)

The methods of reeling from the cocoon and of making sewing-silk were of the most primitive kind. (*e*) The writer has in his possession a specimen of the reeled silk; it was called "tow", and it looks like that material, being coarse, of irregular thickness of fibre, and wholly wanting in luster. By a laborious hand-process, this was converted into sewing-silk of fair quality; but only half the amount in weight could thus be successfully manipulated; the rest was a knotted, irregular refuse, barely available in making homespun garments. The sewing-silk or "twist" had a low reputation as compared with that imported from Italy. It was put up in small parcels, called "sticks", containing a definite number of yards. Twenty-five skeins were tied in a bunch, and four bunches were

---

a Holmes's American Annals; Cambridge, 1805, vol. ii, p. 470.
b Memorial of Windham and Tolland, p. 4.
c Rush Letter, p. 18.
d Memor. Windham and Tolland, p. 5.
e A full account of these processes will be found in Cobb's Manual, pp. 121–124.

fastened together; this gave a merchantable package of 100 skeins—a unit of trade that was used in barter and took the place of currency. Very little money was used at that time in the state, and the sewing-silk became the "circulating medium". An act of the legislature defined the length of the skein, and was enforced by penalty, as follows:

> Any person or persons who shall offer for sale any sewing-silk, unless each skein consists of twenty threads, each thread of the length of two yards, shall forfeit the sum of seven dollars to any person who shall prosecute the same to effect. (*a*)

Naturally enough, when the medium of trade had thus acquired an artificial value, it became the interest of each producer of this currency to debase it. This was effected in two ways: by making the thread as fine as possible, so as to get the greatest length out of a given weight of material, and by putting only half the length in a skein and calling it a "half-skein". The object of the latter device was to give an opportunity, as the silk went from hand to hand, of passing half-skeins as whole ones. The chance of this immoral advantage made the half-skeins the more popular currency. (*b*) An improvement in the spinning wheel was patented in the year 1800 by Horace Hanks; it was known as the "double wheel-head". This gave the spindle an increased speed of 145 turns to one as compared with the old-fashioned machinery.

Connecticut's industry at the close of the last century included the manufacture of "some silk buttons, handkerchiefs, ribands, and stuffs," but of a much less value than the sewing-silk. In 1790 the manufacture of silk laces was begun at Ipswich, Massachusetts; (*c*) it lasted for many years, and the product rose to 41,979 yards of laces, edgings, etc. Silk shoes are also mentioned as an item of some importance among the early manufactures of Massachusetts. These branches of industry were gradually supplanted by others. The change at Ipswich is thus described:

> The machinery which once turned out thread and silk laces, those non-conducers to health and comfort, is now profitably employed in manufacturing cotton and other useful fabrics. (*d*)

The making of fringes, coach laces, and tassels at Philadelphia, Pennsylvania, began in the year 1793. It was expanded in 1815 to include silk trimmings of various kinds, by Wm. H. Horstmann. (*e*)

---

a The Silk Industry of the United States from 1766 to 1874, by A. T. Lilly; New York, 1875, p. 3.

b Ibid., p. 5.   *c* Hayward's Massachusetts Gazetteer, p. 179.

d Ibid.; the date of this remark is 1847.

e American Silk Industry Chronologically Arranged, by Franklin Allen, New York, 1876, p. 5.

There is a record of fresh exertions by Mr. Aspinwall, in 1790, to extend the planting of the mulberry in Pennsylvania, New York and New Jersey. (*a*) During the war of 1812 Samuel Chidsey, of Scipio, Cayuga county, New York, made and sold 600 pounds of sewing-silk, the product of native worms. (*b*)

A small mill, 12 feet square, was built by Rodney and Horatio Hanks, in 1810, at Mansfield, Connecticut, to manufacture sewing-silk by water-power. A larger attempt of the same kind was made by the same persons, associated with others, at Gurleyville, Connecticut, on the Fenton river, in 1814. Neither of these enterprises met the hopes of their projectors; but in 1821 Rodney Hanks built another mill at Mansfield, which was kept in operation for seven years. The Mansfield Silk Company, formed in 1829 by Alfred Lilly, Joseph Conant, William A. Fisk, William Atwood, Storrs Hovey, and Jesse Bingham, undertook the same kind of business, with far better though not complete success; their throwing machinery, devised by Edmund Golding from plans with which he had been familiar in England, being serviceable, though somewhat crude.

The insuperable difficulty during all this period arose from the bad reeling of domestic silk. No power-driven machinery that has ever been devised is capable of making a good uniform thread from such reeled silk as was then produced in the households of New England, although, as has been stated, a fair sewing-silk could be extracted from it by hand-work, with great loss of raw material. The bad reeling which was customary seems more remarkable since several excellent kinds of hand-reels, with a traverse, had been constructed by inventors of that day. Among the makers or describers of improved reels may be mentioned Jonathan H. Cobb, Gideon B. Smith, J. d'Homergue, Jonathan Dennis, jr., Seth W. Cheney, Eliphalet Snow, and Nathan Rixford. The Mansfield Silk Company sought to avoid this difficulty by reeling for themselves, with a power-driven reel. Success attended this effort, and with good reeling "the native silk was found to be of superior quality and strength, winding and doubling with greater facility and less waste than China or Brussia silk". (*c*) The comparative cost is not stated.

In December, 1825, the subject of silk culture began to receive national attention, being brought before Congress by a resolution of inquiry introduced by Mr. Miner, of Pennsylvania, and referred to

---

a Rush letter, p. 17.
b *Ibid.*, p. 18.
c Lilly, Silk Industry, p. 6.

the committee on agriculture. During the following spring the committee reported favorably, presenting, among other arguments on the subject, a statement that the value of silk goods imported in 1825 was nearly twice as great as the export of breadstuffs. The report included a resolution directing the Secretary of the Treasury to cause to be prepared a well-digested manual on the growth and manufacture of silk. Inquiries for information upon the subject were sent out by the secretary, Richard Rush, in 1826; and from the replies and other material, a manual was constructed, entitled "Letter from the Secretary of the Treasury," (*a*) dated February 7, 1828. Six thousand copies were printed by order of Congress. This manual became known as the "Rush Letter"; it contains 220 pages, beside illustrations of machinery, and is a carefully executed work. Other documents relating to silk culture were received and published by Congress at this time, among which were two that have been previously referred to, viz, "Memorial from sundry inhabitants of the counties of Windham and Tolland, state of Connecticut, praying for the aid of government in the cultivation of the mulberry tree and of silk," and an elaborate "Treatise on the culture of silk in Germany, by Count von Hazzi, of Munich" (*b*).

A report presented to the House in 1830 by the committee on agriculture, included two interesting letters from Peter S. Du Ponceau, LL. D., who accompanied Baron Steuben to this country in 1777, and afterward rose to eminence at Philadelphia in public affairs and in studies of philology and law. Essays on American silk by John d'Homergue also formed part of the report. The essays and letters contain much useful information, largely drawn from the experience of their authors in raising silk. The report proposed a grant to M. d'Homergue of $40,000 for the establishment of a normal school of filature at Philadelphia, to supply gratuitous instruction to 60 young men for two years in the details of reeling, dyeing, and manufacturing silk. M. d'Homergue was to be authorized meantime to travel through the different states and teach the art to farmers and others. A bill containing these propositions was brought to a vote in 1832 and was defeated by a small majority. The subject was again referred to the committee on agriculture, which in 1835 made an adverse report on constitutional grounds. In the following year the matter was referred to the committee on manufactures, which reported in 1837; this report contained a letter from

---

a Doc. 158, Twentieth Congress, first session.
b Doc. 226, *idem.*

Hon. Andrew T. Judson, of Connecticut, which furnishes more definite statements than can be readily found elsewhere as to the spread of silk enterprises at this period. Finally the committee on agriculture again reported April 20, 1838. This last report, which was very elaborate, declared that the "silk bill" was defeated because the "ingenuity and experience of our countrymen now render it unnecessary, believing as they do that the recent improvements in reeling will do more in a few weeks than the establishment of many normal schools on the old plan will do in many years". (a) The committee recommended that all public lands in the United States be leased gratuitously wherever the cultivation of the mulberry and the sugar-beet was undertaken thereon.

During the pendency of the bill in 1830 Mr. Du Ponceau started a small filature of 10 reels and 20 operatives on his own account, under M. d'Homergue's direction, at Philadelphia. Among the first fruits of his labor were two flags of American silk; these were presented respectively to the legislature of Pennsylvania and to the United States House of Representatives. About 60 pounds of the silk prepared at this filature was submitted to different manufacturers, who reported upon it as of excellent quality. The subject of silk culture gained the public ear, and the legislatures of several states passed bills for the encouragement of the new industry. The tendency during the years immediately preceding 1837 was toward venturous enterprises, and silk culture presented an attractive field. A peculiar variety of the mulberry tree, believed to possess many advantages as compared with the white mulberry, was brought to public notice, and a speculation was started of such rapid and extensive growth that in a few years it overshadowed all silk enterprises and changed the whole course of the industry.

Gideon B. Smith, of Baltimore, claimed to have owned the first *Morus multicaulis* tree in the United States; it was planted in 1826.(b) Dr. Felix Pascalis, of New York, (afterward editor of a publication called *The Silk Culturist*) called attention to the supposed merits of this plant in *The American Journal of Science*, July, 1830, and described its introduction into Europe by Samuel Perrottet, of the Linnæan Society of Paris. Dr. Pascalis predicted that by its culture two crops of silk could be raised in a season; the prediction was soon afterward verified. The tree was said to grow with marvelous rapidity, developing large, thin, tender, and succulent leaves, in pro-

---

a Report to Twenty-fifth Congress, second session.
b Clarke's Mulberry and Silkworm, p. 121.

fusion. It could be propagated easily by cuttings; it could be cultivated as a shrub; its leaves formed the choicest and most nutritious food for silkworms. All the agricultural literature in the country soon became suffused with descriptions of this wonderful tree. In 1831 the Massachusetts legislature ordered the preparation of a manual on silk culture. The work was performed by Jonathan H. Cobb, a silk manufacturer at Dedham, Massachusetts. The manual was printed in the same year; it passed through at least four editions, and spread the merits of the *Morus multicaulis* throughout the New England states.

The following bounties were authorized by legislatures :

Maine : 5 cents on every pound of cocoons raised. Connecticut, act of 1832 : $1 on every one hundred transplanted mulberry trees two years old; 50 cents on every pound of silk reeled on an improved reel.

Vermont, act of 1835: 10 cents on every pound of cocoons raised.

Massachusetts, act of 1836: $1 on every ten pounds of cocoons raised in the state; $1 for every pound of silk reeled and thrown; 50 cents for every pound of silk reeled but not thrown.

New Jersey: 16 cents per pound for cocoons, and 50 cents per pound for reeled silk.

There were similar acts in New York, Pennsylvania, Georgia, Indiana, and probably in other states. The largest quantity of cocoons raised by any one claimant for bounty in Massachusetts was 615 pounds. (*a*) The legislation of that state was regarded as quite liberal. (*b*) Beside all this, there were premiums paid by counties, by fairs, and by stock companies interested in silk growing. A grant of 262 acres of land, owned by the United States, at Greenbush, New York, was made to G. B. Clark, of New York city, on condition that he should plant 100,000 mulberry trees, and provide sufficient silkworms to consume all the foliage thereof. Certainly the new business did not lack encouragement.

A national silk convention was held at Baltimore in December, 1838; a silk convention in New Jersey, February, 1839; in New York, at Albany, February, 1839; in Connecticut, April, 1839; and there were many other gatherings of the kind. The list of stock companies formed for raising and manufacturing silk at this time is very long; their lives were very short. Many of them were slenderly equipped, in both knowledge and resources. Seven are named in

---

a American Silk Grower, p. 267.
b Cobb's Manual, p. 47.

Massachusetts, six in Pennsylvania, nearly as many in neighboring states, and a few at the west. A United States Silk Society was organized at the national convention. The number of private individuals engaged in silk raising cannot be estimated. In Burlington, New Jersey, says a writer of the day, "you can scarcely go into a house but you find the inmates engaged in feeding worms." (a)

The literature of the period on this subject was abundant and various. In the following list the titles of some of the more noted publications are presented:

Authors—JAMES MEASE, M. D., of Philadelphia: *Letter to Secretary Rush;* U. S. Twentieth Congress, House Doc. 158. JOHN CLARKE: *Treatise on the Mulberry and Silkworm;* Philadelphia. JONATHAN H. COBB: *Manual.* PETER DELABIGARRE: *A Treatise on Silkworms;* New York. PETER S. DU PONCEAU AND JOHN D'HOMERGUE: Philadelphia. GIDEON B. SMITH (Ed. *American Farmer*): *Manual;* Baltimore: also Ed. *Journal of the American Silk Society and Rural Economist;* 2 vols., Baltimore, 1840. JONATHAN DAVIS: *Manual.* WARD CHENEY & BROS.: *American Silk-Grower and Farmers' Manual;* Philadelphia. THOMAS G. FESSENDEN: *The Silk Manual and Farmer* (monthly); Boston. S. BLYDENBURGH: *The Silkworm* (monthly); Albany, New York. FRANKLIN G. COMSTOCK: *Practical Treatise on the Culture of Silk;* Hartford 1835 and 1839; also, *Silk Culturist;* Hartford. E. P. ROBERTS (Ed. *Farmer and Gardener*): *Manual;* Baltimore. WM. KENRICK: *American Silk-Growers' Guide.* DR. FELIX PASCALIS: *Instructions for Silkworm Nurseries, and Culture of the Mulberry Tree;* also, *Silk Culturist* (periodical); New York. SAMUEL WHITMARSH: *Eight Years' Experience and Observation in the Culture of the Mulberry Tree and the Care of the Silkworm;* Northampton, Mass. EDMUND MORRIS: *The Silk Record* (periodical); Burlington, N. J. JUDGE BUELL: *The Albany Cultivator* (monthly); Albany, N. Y. EDMUND RUFFIN: *The Farmers' Register* (periodical); Richmond, Va. ANNUAL REPORTS OF THE AMERICAN INSTITUTE (yearly); New York, N. Y. GENERAL HENRY ALEX. SCAMMEL DEARBORN: *Internal Improvements and Commerce of the West;* Boston, 1839. JOHN S. SKINNER: *Christmas Gift to Young Agriculturists;* Washington, D. G., 1841.

London works distributed in this country.—SAMUEL PULLEIN: *The Culture of Silk for the American Colonies, and the Culture of Mulberry Trees;* London, 1758. DR. DIONYSIUS LARDNER: *Treatise on the Origin, Improvements, and Present State of the Silk Manufacture;* London.

Translations.—M. MORIN: *Art of Raising and Feeding Silkworms, and of Cultivating the Mulberry Tree;* Boston, 1836. JULIEN STANISLAUS: *Résumé des Principaux Traités Chinois sur la Culture des Muriers et l'Éducation des Vers à Soie;* Paris, 1838 (Translated by Peter Force, mayor of Washington, D. C., 1838). DESLONGCHAMPS: *Essai sur des Muriers et des Vers d Soie; Paris,* 1824. SIGNOR TENELLI (Doctor of Civil Law in the University of Pavia): *Hints on the Cultivation of the Mulberry.* M. BONAFOUX (Director of the Royal Gardens at Turin): *Essai sur des Muriers, etc.* COUNT VON HAZZI, Munich: *Translation of Essay;* U. S. 20th Congress, House Doc. 226. COUNT S. DANDOLO; *Manual for the Culture of Silk,* abridged: Washington, 1828. DE LA BROUSSE: *Des Muriers et*

---

a American Silk Grower, p. 54.

de l'Éducation de Vers à Soie; Nismes, 1789: abridged translation by W. H. Vernon, Boston, 1828.

To the foregoing should be added the various reports of Congressional committees, and especially that of the committee on agriculture in April, 1838, which gives an account of the merits of the *multicaulis* mulberry.

This literature, so far as our native authors are concerned, is in one respect peculiar. Its errors lie all in a single direction. The silk production in past years is often overstated; the probable yield from trees, eggs and cocoons is often overestimated; plentiful profits are calculated; but the the mistake of understating is nowhere made.

Gradually, but at an increasing rate of velocity, the tide of speculation rose. Large as were the anticipated profits of producing silk, they were insignificant as compared with the fortunes to be made by raising the new mulberry tree. Orchards of it were planted in every state in the Union. At least 300,000 trees were sold at Burlington, New Jersey, by September, 1838,(*a*) and all that were growing there could have been sold at 40 to 50 cents apiece, if owners had been willing to take that price. The demand raised the value abroad, so that trees which had been worth 8 to $12\frac{1}{2}$ cents each in France could not be bought there on a remittance of less than 18 to 30 cents.(*b*) In December, 1838, sales were made in Boston at $1 per tree, but the owners withdrew most of the lot, being dissatisfied with the prices obtained.(*c*) Trees of a single season's growth were sometimes sold at $5 each.(*d*) A belief in the profit of silk culture was, of course, the basis of the demand for the tree, and a table was published showing that in the actual experience of fourteen people, an average of $1,000 per acre had been obtained, at $4 per pound of silk.(*e*) But the value of the trees became greater than that of the silk which they could by any possibility be the means of producing. A farmer in Belchertown, who planted $1,000 worth of the *Morus multicaulis* in 1838 on three-quarters of an acre, sold the trees the next year for $6,000.(*f*) The sales in a single week in Pennsylvania exceeded $300,000, and in many cases the same trees were sold two or three times at advancing prices.(*g*) In other instances, the proceeds of 15 acres were $32,500; of 2 acres, $4,000; of 10 acres, $38,000. The exact procedure at one of these sales is given as follows :

---

a American Silk Grower, p. 60.
b Ibid., p. 78.
c Ibid., p. 148.
d Lilly, Silk Industry, p. 8.
e American Silk Grower, p. 244.
f Ibid., p. 222.
g Morris' Silk Farmer, September, 1839.

Annexed is a correct statement of the number, prices and proceeds of the *Morus multicaulis*, sold September 18. 1839, at auction, at the Highfield Cocoonery, Germantown, Pennsylvania. The trees were sold as they stood in the ground; those under 12 inches to be rejected. Owing to a thin soil and close planting, the sizes of trees were generally small and the branches few; the average height, according to an estimate made on the ground, being about 2½ feet. The purchasers were mostly from a distance, the largest portion being from Illinois, Missouri and other Western States. 260,000 trees were sold at prices ranging from 17 to 37½ cents per tree, averaging 31 23-100 cents per tree, or 12½ cents per foot in length of stalk. The total sale was $81,218 75.(*a*)

The testimony of an eye-witness at Northampton in 1839 is that :

Mr. Samuel Whitmarsh and Dr. Daniel Stebbins were rejoicing over the purchase of a dozen *multicaulis* cuttings, not more than 2 feet long, and of the thickness of a pipe-stem, for $25. "They are worth $60," exclaimed the doctor, in his enthusiasm.(*b*)

The discovery was made that cuttings with the eyes or buds were sufficient for planting an orchard :

On Friday last the steamboat Alabama took up to Baltimore 22,000 mulberry switches (*Morus multicaulis*) from 6 to 8 feet in length; the value of which, at the lowest calculation, based upon actual sales all through the country, cannot be less than $45,000. The number of eyes or buds on these 22,000 switches is ascertained by carefully counting them, to be 2,254,000, which, according to prevailing prices, would be considered cheap at 2 to 2½ cents apiece. The whole were raised on 15 acres of such land as would be considered well sold at $10 an acre in ordinary situations.(*c*)

The bubble burst in 1839. Silk culturists and manufacturers had everywhere been swept into the rising current. As for the tree speculators, it is related that one, who had been among the most successful, sent an agent to France with $80,000 to buy trees and cuttings in the winter of 1838–'39.

Before the whole of his purchase had arrived the crisis had come. The nurseryman had failed for so large a sum that he could never reckon up his indebtedness, and the next spring his *multicaulis* trees were offered in vain to the neighboring farmers at $1 a hundred for pea-brush.(*d*)

Agriculturists were angry and vociferous over their losses and pulled up most of their mulberry orchards.

In every village, numerous gardens and outlots might be seen planted with *multicaulis;* in 1843 these trees had become a worthless incumbrance, and in many instances were rooted out and thrown away.(*e*)

---

a Hazard's United States Statistical Register, 1839.
b The Silk Industry in America, by L. P. Brockett, M. D.; New York, 1876, p 39.
c American Silk Grower, p. 287.
d Brockett: Silk Industry, p. 40.
e Historical Collections of Pennsylvania, by Sherman Day; Philadelphia, 1843, p. 167.

For a few years after the collapse of the *multicaulis,* some interest was taken in the hardier *Morus alba.* Two trees of one season's growth, raised by Elder Sharp, of North Windham, Connecticut, were sold standing in his nursery in August, 1842, at auction, for $106 and $100. Further sales were withheld because the bidding was not considered sufficiently spirited.(*a*) In 1844, a blight of a general character, to which even the hardy white mulberry yielded, gave the finishing blow, and silk culture in America ceased to exist.

Meanwhile, step by step, improvements had been effected in the manufacture of silk goods. As early as 1828, Toerhoven Bros., of Philadelphia, had invented a machine for reeling, doubling, and twisting at once.(*b*) A later invention, by Gamaliel Gay,(*c*) of Poughkeepsie, New York, had a similar object—to reel silk and to make sewing-thread by one operation—and was highly praised by his contemporaries.(*d*) But success did not lie in this direction. Improvements in the machinery for winding, doubling, and spinning, which are mostly credited to Nathan Rixford, of Mansfield, Connecticut, were introduced about 1838, and proved of permanent value. One of the most important of these is the "friction roller." This device avoids the unequal twist in the thread, which otherwise arises from the increase of diameter as the wound silk accumulates upon a bobbin.(*e*)

There are the following statistics of production in Massachusetts for the year 1837: value of sewing-silk manufactured at Dedham, in this year, $10,000; at Northampton, sewing-silk, 6,100 pounds, valued at $41,500; at Quincy and Reading, coach lace, value at latter place, $6,000; Roxbury, fringes and tassels, $15,000; total in Massachusetts, raw silk, $952; sewing-silk, $150,477; hands employed, 156.(*f*) In 1830 the manufacture of silk fringes, tassels, and the like was begun in New York city; this business, including many different kinds of trimmings, is now one of the largest branches of the silk industry, and is more extensively developed in New York than elsewhere, though for many years Philadelphia held pre-eminence. The machinery in use in 1830 in the silk factories at

---

a Lilly: Silk Industry, p. 9.
b Rush Letter, p. 169.
c Mr. Gay was also the inventor of a silk power-loom, said to be capable of weaving silk more rapidly than cotton of equal fineness could be woven. Looms of this kind were put in operation about the year 1835 in silk factories at Providence, Rhode Island, and Nantucket, Massachusetts.—Bishop, ii, p. 392.
d Clarke's Mulberry and Silkworm, p. 116.
e Allen's Chronology, p. 9.
f Hayward's Massachusetts Gazeteer, p. 135.

Mansfield, Connecticut, consisted of 32 doubling spindles, 84 for throwing, 32 for soft-silk winding, two broad looms, and one for fringe silk. (*a*)

In addition to the preceding details, the dates of starting the silk manufacture in various localities may be briefly stated as follows:

1829. Baltimore, Maryland; ribbons.
1834. Boston, Massachusetts; dress trimmings.
1834-1838. Florence, Massachusetts; sewing-silk.
1835. Dedham, Massachusetts; sewing-silk.
1838. South Manchester, Connecticut; general silk manufacture.
1838. Windsor Locks, Connecticut; sewing-silk.
1840. Paterson, New Jersey; general silk manufacture.
1840. Canton, Massachusetts; sewing-silk.
1842. Newark, New Jersey; sewing-silk.
1843. Philadelphia, Pennsylvania; sewing-silk.
1848. Skinnerville, afterward moved to Holyoke, Mass.; sewing-silk.
1849. Watertown, Connecticut; sewing-silk.
1852. Philadelphia, Pennsylvania; ribbons.
1863. Rockville, Connecticut; sewing-silk.
1865. Trenton, New Jersey; coach lace.
1865. New York, New York; general silk manufacture.
1866. Willimantic, Connecticut; sewing-silk.
1866. Oneida, New York; sewing-silk.
1868. Hoboken, New Jersey; silk dress goods.
1870. San Francisco, California; sewing-silk and fringe-silk.
1871. Brooklyn, New York; silk laces.
1872. College Point, Long Island, New York; ribbons.
1874. Wortendyke, New Jersey; silk handkerchiefs and dress goods.
1875. Town of Union, New Jersey; silk dress goods.

It has been already mentioned that the foundation of the present silk manufacture was laid in the making of sewing-silk; this is not only true of the business in general, it is part of the individual history of many leading concerns. Each of the successful enterprises has started from very small beginnings and with very slender resources. A close competition, at first with foreign, afterward with domestic rivals, has compelled experiment in new directions, and, coupled in most branches of the business with constantly changing fashions, has required frequent alterations and improvements in machinery. In the course of a recent attempt to ascertain the percentage of decline in the prices of silk goods during the last two decades of years, the writer constantly encountered the fact that very few of the kinds of goods in the market now are like

---

a Historical Collections of Connecticut, by John W. Barber; Hartford, 1836, p. 550.

those that were made ten years ago, and scarcely any are precisely comparable with those of 1860. Many of the experiments in making new goods met partial or complete failure at first, but were again and again renewed till the difficulties were overcome; and of these most interesting trials there is little record. A description of the enterprises, aside from the difficulty of giving fair credit to each of the pioneers in different localities, would require a series of biographical sketches beyond the plan of the present work. For these and other reasons it is not practicable to state the exact dates when the various branches of the industry were first undertaken; but the following general statements may be of service :

The beginnings of the manufacture of sewing-silk by machinery have been already described; the production of "machine-twist"— a kind of thread suited for use on the sewing-machine, and first adapted to that purpose in February, 1852—gave a great impetus to this branch of the trade. Since then the sewings and twist manufacture, keeping pace with the rapidly increasing use of sewing-machines, has wholly freed itself from foreign rivalry, but suffers from the keenest of home competition. Manufactures of spun silk (which now include almost every kind of silk goods) were begun at South Manchester, Connecticut, about twenty-five years ago. Ribbons began to be made to supply deficiences in imported invoices as early as 1861; their manufacture here was much stimulated during the war of the Rebellion by the high price of gold, which checked their import. Plain gros-grain dress silks were made to some extent by different manufacturers before 1866, when the business was organized in New Jersey; its most rapid growth is since 1876. The recent developement of this branch of the industry is largely due to improvements in the processes of "finishing," which is carried on by several firms as their sole business. Brocaded silks and satins were attempted on a large scale earlier than plain gros-grain, and were produced in several factories when that was confined to a few. The business of printing Asiatic pongees preceded the regular manufacture of handkerchiefs, which was of slow growth till 1876, when it received a remarkable impulse from the Centennial Exhibition. Hair nets and spot nets were largely produced in 1868; a lace covering for buttons was made on a lace machine in 1869; these undertakings paved the way for the manufacture of silk laces, which was established at Brooklyn, New York, in 1871. The making of trimmings of all kinds forms a very large branch of the silk industry, but this high position has been acquired mostly within the last ten years, although certain classes of trimmings were produced before the present century, and have since been made continuously. Silk tapestry and the like are just emerging from the experimental stage, which velvet has not yet quitted.

Throughout the silk manufacture, the condition—or rather, the character—of the raw material is a potent factor. The machinery of American silk mills is driven at the highest speed compatible with good work. Such speed is often needed to catch the demand of a short-lived fashion, and it proves generally profitable by economizing labor. For use on the swiftest spindles and looms, raw silk of the most uniform character is required. For many years the Asiatic supply was unsatisfactory, while the European was too costly to be used at a profit. An important effort was made in 1840–'41 to secure the better preparation of China silk for this market. The chief point was to obtain better reeling or re-reeling by means of a winding-frame moved by a crank, in place of direct winding by hand from stationary bamboo sticks. In re-reeling, also, the sizes of the fibre were to be sorted. Improved reels made by Mr. Rixford, and provided with a traverse attachment, were sent to China. Owing to oriental prejudices, the attempt was at that time unsuccessful. About thirteen years afterward the effort was renewed, and the first re-reeled China silk was brought to New York in 1854. For a while the work was well done, but the Chinese became careless about it, and the re-reeled silk deteriorated so much that its importation ceased. A third effort to secure better reeling in China was made in 1867 and met with more permanent success,(a) though at best the work there falls far short of the highest standards. Imperfect reeling in the United States had destroyed the market for our native silk and retarded our manufactures; imperfect reeling in China was for even a longer term the chief obstacle to improvement, all progress being hampered by defects in the raw material. Among the causes of rapid advance in the arts of manufacture during very recent years, improvement in the quality of raw silk, especially from Japan, holds a promiment place.

The use of Asiatic silk in this country began with the earliest successful manufacture, about 1829, the first importation of the material being in 1828. Eventually the receipts of raw silk became a correct index of the amount of silk manufacture in this country, but there was a period during which the import was nearly balanced by an export, the Asiatic silk from around Cape Horn merely passing through our ports on its way to Europe. For instance, the following were the values of imports and exports of raw silk from September 30, 1831, to September 30, 1836 :

Year.	Import.	Export.
1831	$88,557	$134,376
1832	48,938	48,800
1833	135,348	66,456
1834	78,706	139,256
1835	10,715	4,114
1836	37,507	....
Total	$399,771	$393,002

Before taking the import of raw silk as our guide to the amount of manufacture, we may consider a few statistics from other sources. The manufacture of sewing-silk in the United States in 1844 is reported as "396,790 pounds, exclusive of what was used and made in families; of that quantity 176,210 pounds were made in Connecticut." (a) There are good reasons for regarding these figures as greatly in excess of the actual production. The census of 1850 showed a much smaller amount of manufacture, and was doubtless nearer the facts, the totals given being of sewing-silk, value $1,209,-426, silk cloth, $17,050; fringe, gimp and tassels, $583,000; total, $1,809,476. In 1855 there were made in Massachusetts, in the three counties of Hampshire, Essex and Norfolk, 44,000 pounds of sewing silk, worth $300,000. "That quantity was exclusive of fringes and tassels, made chiefly at Roxbury, to the value of $433,000, and ribbons and dress trimmings to the value of $38,000 by one establishment at Newton." As the silk manufacture of Connecticut was then larger than that of any other state, and there was a considerable amount in Pennsylvania and New Jersey, the value of the whole amount of silk goods made in that year certainly exceeded $3,000,000. For the year ending June 30, 1860, the census returns give a total of silk goods valued at $6,607,771. It is noteworthy that the number of pounds of sewings and twist is 89 per cent. of the whole number of pounds of raw silk said to be consumed as material, and that the latter is in excess of the estimated import. The value of silk goods made in 1870, according to that year's census, was $12,210,662. The value in 1880, net, in finished goods, was $34,519,723.

In the following table the imports of raw silk are given from 1843 to 1880, inclusive, according to the records of the United States bureau of statistics, as to the value and number of pounds, except where the pounds are estimated; and the receipts of raw silk at New York and San Francisco are also presented in number of bales and cases since 1850, according to the records of the Silk Association of America:

---

a Census of 1860; Introduction, p. ci.

SILK MANUFACTURE IN THE UNITED STATES.

Imports of Raw Silk by Fiscal Years.

Year	Pounds.	Value.	Number of bales and cases at New York and San Francisco.
1843	17,898	$53,250	
1844	59,192	172,593	
1845	62,657	208,454	
1846	68,938	216,647	
1847	a 100,034	250,086	
1848	a 189,319	354,973	
1849	a 144,204	384,533	
1850	a 120,010	401,385	
1851	a 144,144	456,449	
1852	a 119,604	378,747	1,540
1853	a 234,648	722,981	2,527
1854	a 305,523	1,099,339	5,604
1855	a 237,968	751,617	3,776
1856	a 304,994	991,234	4,425
1857	a 190,737	953,734	3,107
1858	a 422,658	1,542,195	5,037
1859	a 388,507	1,619,157	3,859
1860	a 297,877	1,340,676	5,241
1861	a 361,891	1,507,876	3,837
1862	a 132,460	489,526	1,008
1863	a 250,740	1,018,468	2,667
1864	407,935	2,057,964	2,429
1865	290,021	1,193,870	2,093
1866	567,904	3,437,900	3,977
1867	401,983	2,469,001	2,252
1868	512,449	2,921,573	4,938
1869	720,045	3,318,496	5,946
1870	583,589	3,017,958	5,263
1871	1,100,281	5,789,392	8,164
1872	1,063,809	5,625,020	9,203
1873	1,150,430	6,460,621	11,129
1874	794,837	3,854,008	7,862
1875	1,101,681	4,504,306	9,768
1876	1,354,991	5,424,408	11,060
1877	1,186,170	6,792,937	10,640
1878	1,182,750	5,103,084	10,190
1879	1,889,776	8,371,025	15,949
1880	2,562,236	12,024,699	21,741

As it will be of interest to make some comparisons between the importation of silk goods and their manufacture, tables are herewith given of the imports. The first of the tables is from the records of the United States bureau of statistics, by fiscal years, giving the values of the whole imports of silk manufactures into the United States since 1825. Nine or ten per cent. of these imported goods *in the earlier years* was exported. The second table gives values of the same classes of imports by calendar years at the port of New York, and it may be accepted as representing for those years 95 per cent. of the whole.

Imports of silk manufactures by fiscal years.

Year.	Value.	Year.	Value.	Year.	Value.	Year.	Value.
1825	$10,271,527	1839	$21,638,828	1853	$30,492,024	1867	$18,357,052
1826	8,104,837	1840	9,526,988	1854	34,785,632	1868	16,908,532
1827	6,545,245	1841	15,256,907	1855	24,366,556	1869	22,288,069
1828	7,608,614	1842	9,415,370	1856	30,226,582	1870	23,870,142
1829	7,048,628	1843	2,663,410	1857	27,800,319	1871	32,341,001
1830	5,774,019	1844	7,088,406	1858	21,229,358	1872	36,448,618
1831	10,904,398	1845	8,713,326	1859	28,080,366	1873	29,890,035
1832	9,094,566	1846	8,827,307	1860	32,961,120	1874	23,996,782
1833	9,174,199	1847	10,821,722	1861	23,657,209	1875	24,380,923
1834	2,609,349	1848	14,582,743	1862	7,588,376	1876	23,745,967
1835	16,597,983	1849	13,791,282	1863	12,890,760	1877	21,830,159
1836	22,862,177	1850	17,679,187	1864	20,597,728	1878	19,837,972
1837	14,115,171	1851	25,829,692	1865	8,489,143	1879	24,013,398
1838	9,812,338	1852	21,623,646	1866	28,308,606	1880	32,188,690

Imports of silk manufactures at the Port of New York, by calendar years.

Year.	Value.	Year.	Value.	Year.	Value.
1851	$23,548,774	1861	$12,298,863	1871	$33,899,719
1852	22,519,223	1862	10,942,938	1872	32,677,749
1853	33,089,081	1863	14,761,186	1873	24,379,322
1854	27,931,659	1864	14,621,202	1874	23,292,351
1855	23,269,544	1865	18,393,698	1875	23,168,118
1856	29,081,416	1866	22,902,864	1876	21,192,386
1857	27,465,192	1867	16,434,524	1877	19,922,741
1858	17,632,843	1868	18,903,232	1878	20,042,730
1859	31,877,863	1869	22,064,312	1879	25,830,829
1860	34,330,321	1870	26,731,275	1880	33,305,460

The following table is presented in order to show specifically the classes of silk goods imported during the past ten years, and to facilitate comparison between imports and manufactures as to different kinds of articles:

SILK MANUFACTURE IN THE UNITED STATES.

Imports of silk manufactures at the Port of New York, in the calendar years, specifying articles (a).

Articles.	1880	1879	1878	1877	1876	1875	1874	1873	1872	1871
Total	$33,505,160	$25,930,829	$20,042,730	$19,062,741	$21,192,986	$23,106,118	$23,962,551	$24,379,322	$32,677,740	$33,409,719
Dress Silks	17,695,038	15,104,026	11,834,981	11,978,136	12,707,192	12,620,397	10,581,299	9,764,650	11,080,001	13,650,246
Satins	267,939	202,672	98,219	98,726	41,403	107,501	305,394	11,089,001	264,403	312,060
Crapes	443,236	495,662	87,281	397,906	509,257	470,896	641,390	577,975	459,727	409,287
Pongees	8,205	1,696	594	2,617	10,120	2,629	561			451
Plushes	408,219	125,487	101,196	75,777	68,008	198,722	127,045	221,421	309,465	301,150
Velvets	2,044,139	1,976,133	1,510,240	1,384,450	1,151,427	1,067,181	868,149	1,512,600	1,793,905	
Ribbons	3,563,418	2,190,260	1,826,503	1,936,413	1,687,537	2,684,571	3,190,647	4,780,040	8,307,009	7,915,744
Laces	1,540,802	1,069,969	921,305	1,195,639	1,243,740	1,620,055	1,708,161	1,900,072	2,218,432	2,153,969
Embroideries				2,020	699	1,224	2,644	965	2,025	
Shawls	20,677	11,179	5,519	5,611	5,831	73,963	151	5,345	9,336	14,889
Gloves	228,338	196,884	112,941	41,189	29,612	46,628	24,571	40,396	17,337	31,198
Cravats	93,359	115,441	103,049	55,777	413,669	180,730	113,662		175,742	135,982
Handkerchiefs	64,077	54,628	48,701	49,932	46,294	117,368	38,754	24,562	93,337	30,837
Mantillas					573					
Vestings					2,487	3,606	2,467	53,431	66,621	54,817
Hose	118,859	89,997	48,925	34,128	55,618	46,790	26,958	49,325	34,896	30,309
Threads and yarns	239,072	194,103	50,622	81,704	16,507	11,367	37,808	31,611	51,690	105,565
Braids and bindings	1,646,568	1,342,760	985,993	1,143,737	964,689	1,990,555	1,028,320	1,039,906	1,044,644	962,913
Silk and worsted fabrics	199,654	156,258	136,063	136,194	165,714	421,791	476,561	509,580	707,176	1,061,137
Silk and cotton fabrics	4,751,946	2,662,328	1,961,830	1,962,039	2,094,883	2,312,654	3,576,932	4,064,077	6,253,362	4,566,028
Silk and linen fabrics	943	631	600	3,730	10,316	3,689	3,887	5,511	73,726	389,289

a Compiled by the Secretary of the Silk Association of America, 446 Broome Street, New York.

In comparing the foregoing tables with the statistics of production, it should be noticed that the imports are simply the invoiced values, to which must be added the duties, importers' profits, and other expenses of importation, before the market value here can be ascertained. Making these allowances, it appears probable that the proportion of silk goods in this country, to the whole amount used, is slowly rising, as follows:

Percentage of silk goods made in the United States as compared with whole consumption of such goods in the country.

	Per Cent.
In the fiscal year 1860	13
In the fiscal year 1870	23
In the calendar year 1874	28
In the calendar year 1875	34
In the calendar year 1876	35
In the calendar year 1877	32
In the calendar year 1878	36
In the calendar year 1879	39
In the fiscal year 1880	38

If the foreign invoices are much undervalued, the foregoing calculations must be largely modified. For instance, if the undervaluation of silk goods imported in the census year amounted to twenty per cent., the manufacture of such goods in the United States was only one-third of the consumption.

Within a few years there has been a greater and swifter growth than before in certain lines of silk manufacture, while the remainder has simply held to its annual average. This is shown in the tables that follow; the first giving the figures of production for different kinds of goods; the second and third representing graphically that production, and the importations of specified articles. In the graphic charts the scale is uniform, permitting direct comparison:

SILK MANUFACTURE IN THE UNITED STATES.

Production of finished goods in the United States.

Silk Manufactures.	1874	1875	1876	1877	1878	1879	1875—1880
Total	$16,995,137	$21,993,081	$21,991,480	$16,619,743	$20,701,055	$29,983,620	$84,519,728
Machine Twist	4,848,830	5,535,754	6,301,959	4,126,460	4,809,287	5,891,300	6,097,735
Sewing Silk	917,309	883,079	951,460	349,608	409,123	778,250	776,130
Floss Silk	43,000	42,568	35,428	32,600	87,710	166,565	225,025
Dress Goods	1,409,000	1,412,500	1,350,535	1,712,063	2,460,115	3,826,325	4,115,903
Satins	...	...	...	482,420	1,100,175	1,101,875
Tie Silks and Scarfs	287,967	962,587	679,688	169,950	283,160	547,675	606,675
Millinery Silks	773,974	1,696,127	1,119,441	1,119,081	1,007,125	977,495	801,935
Broad Goods, not above enumerated	...	...	...	236,400	583,635	627,505
Handkerchiefs	213,516	905,115	927,000	1,324,163	2,108,390	3,583,125	3,881,590
Ribbons	2,676,836	4,815,485	4,596,556	3,927,496	4,149,345	5,025,205	6,023,160
Lace	183,000	164,000	2-0,000	156,500	247,355	406,300	437,000
Braids and Bindings	398,730	383,100	315,000	250,400	452,950	828,825	959,685
Fringes, Dress and Cloak Trimmings	2,626,805	2,509,501	2,821,394	2,191,135	2,842,615	3,500,860	4,050,275
Cords, Tassels, Passementerie, and Millinery Trimmings	860,601	870,000	900,000	737,045	808,820	930,540	1,866,575
Upholstery and Military Trimmings	408,000	492,613	554,036	404,700	506,145	947,405	1,392,835
Couch Laces and Carriage Trimmings	...	35,652	24,500	18,040	18,439	33,470	37,510
Fur, Hatters' and Undertakers' Trimmings	...	...	...	...	27,630	62,810	50,605
Embroideries	...	...	...	...	24,079	54,900	...
Silk value in Upholstery and Mixed Goods	...	...	...	...	54,886	129,750	519,643
Foulards	500,000	450,000	472,000	290,000	...	...	...
Silk Hose	...	6,000	3,250	4,500	...	...	...

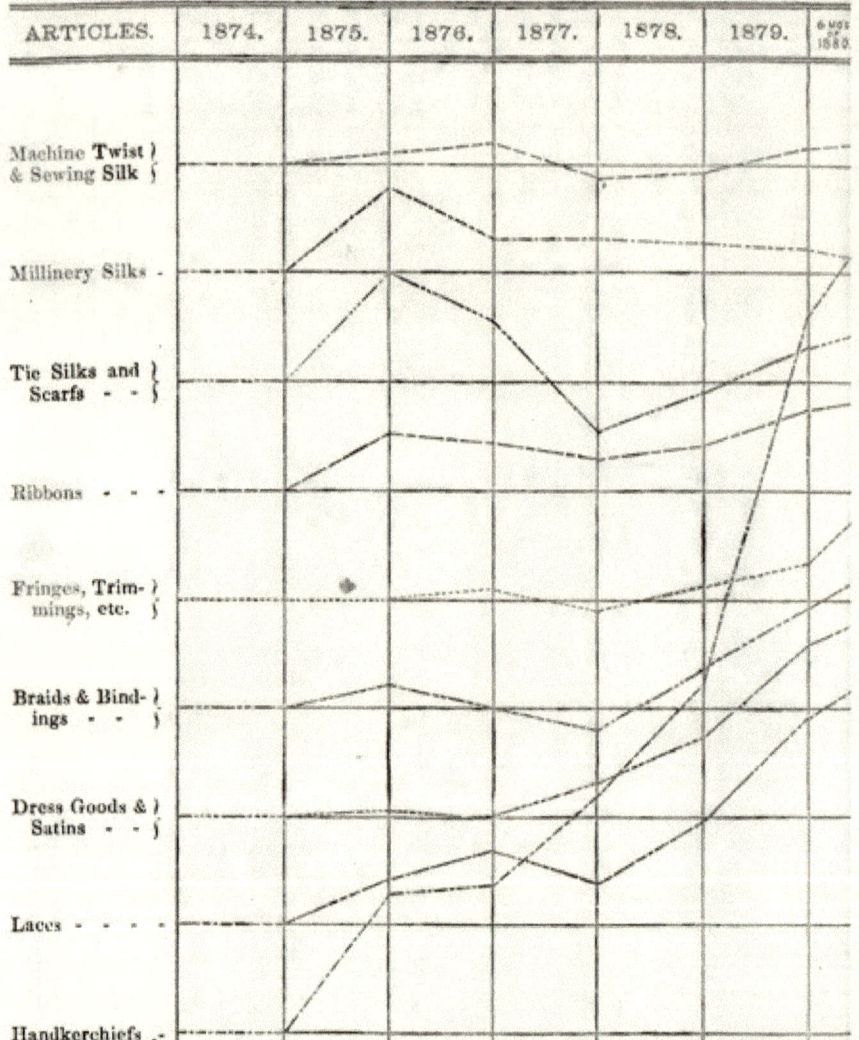

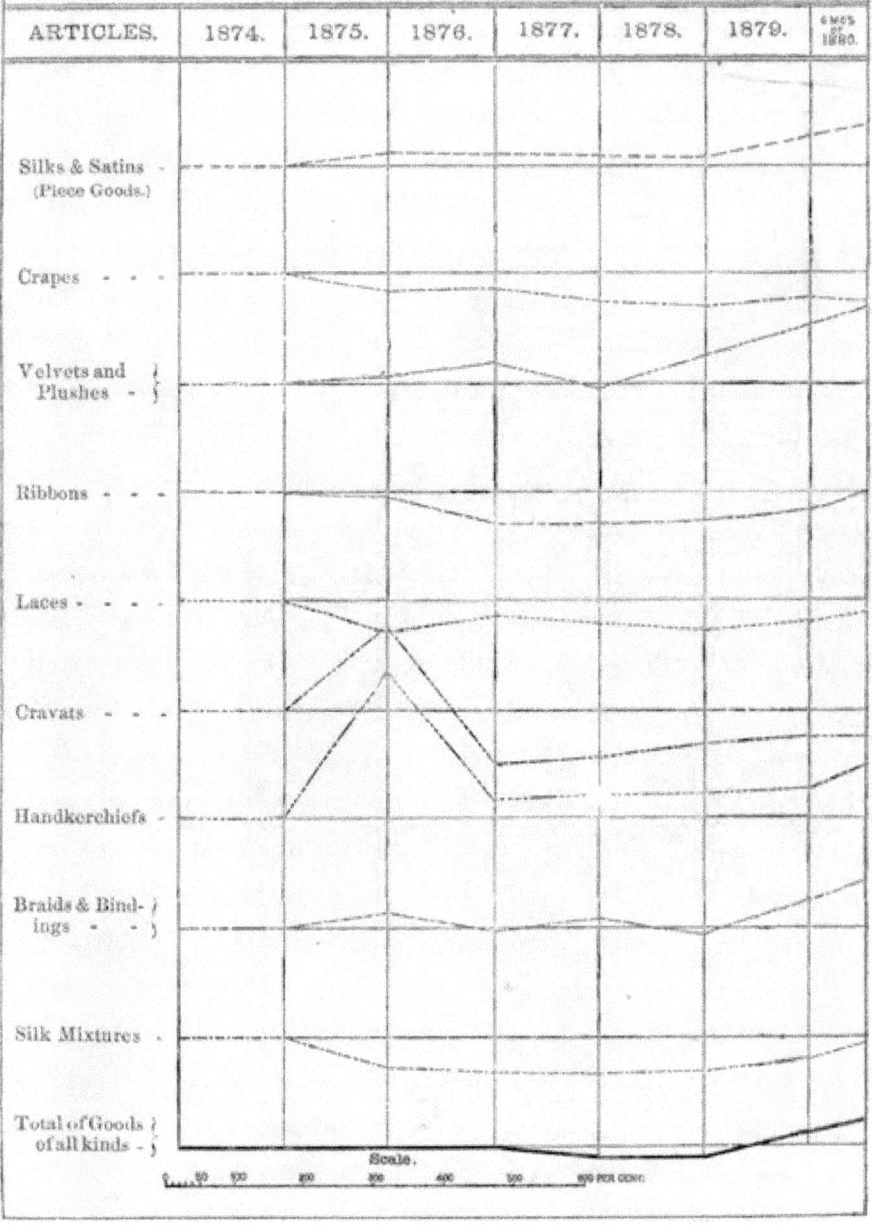

The following are summaries of the census returns of silk manufactures for the years 1850, 1860, 1870, and 1880:

Silk Manufacture, 1850.

Articles.	Establishments.	Hands Employed.			Capital.	Wages.	All Materials.	Products.
		Total.	Males.	Females.				
Total	67	1,728	508	1,220	$678,300	$297,416	$1,093,860	$1,809,476
Sewing Silk	27	829	295	534	428,350	152,712	848,945	1,209,426
Silk Cloth	2	8	3	5	5,600	1,776	11,235	17,050
Fringe, Gimp & Tassels	38	886	205	681	244,350	142,928	233,680	583,000

Silk Manufacture, 1860.

States.	Establishments.	Hands Employed.			Capital.	Wages.
		Total.	Males.	Females.		
The United States	139	5,435	1,585	3,850	$2,926,980	$1,050,224
Connecticut	22	1,137	288	849	997,900	$155,760
Maryland	3	85	22	13	35,800	9,895
Massachusetts	20	781	234	547	330,700	191,720
New Hampshire	2	23	5	18	9,000	3,780
New Jersey	9	716	160	556	207,000	111,462
New York	44	1,159	405	754	323,980	268,024
Ohio	4	25	11	14	11,800	5,782
Pennsylvania	35	1,550	451	1,099	1,010,700	303,780
Vermont						

States.	Materials.		Products.	
	Raw Silk.	All Materials.	Sewing Silk and Twist.	All products.
	Pounds.	Dollars.	Pounds.	Dollars.
The United States	462,965	3,501,777	409,429	6,607,771
Connecticut	151,191	821,807	145,835	1,301,400
Maryland		78,121		89,800
Massachusetts	89,000	814,950	63,900	1,297,050
New Hampshire	6,000	28,000	5,440	36,480
New Jersey	121,634	631,725	107,310	969,700
New York	29,140	644,911	25,444	1,154,294
Ohio		14,300		41,200
Pennsylvania	66,000	927,943	61,500	1,767,845
Vermont				

SILK MANUFACTURE IN THE UNITED STATES.

Silk Manufacture, 1870.

States.	Establishments.	Steam-engines. Horse-power.	Steam-engines. Number.	Water-wheels. Horse-power.	Water-wheels. Number.	Machines. Braiders.	Machines. Looms.	Machines. Looms, hand.	Machines. Spindles.	Machines. Spoolers.	Machines. Winders.	Hands Employed. Total.	Hands Employed. Males above 16.	Hands Employed. Females above 15.	Hands Employed. Youth.	Capital.	Wages.
The United States	86	1,120	48	735	45	90	1,251	188	12,940	2,487	3,088	6,649	1,734	3,529	1,386	$6,931,130	$1,942,286
Connecticut	23	401	11	320	20		236			170	189	1,708	466	1,003	231	1,414,130	869,425
Maryland	1															432,000	154,300
Massachusetts	9	75	6	50						4	520	453	97	286	70	5,000	1,600
New Hampshire	5		16	246	11		236	186	8,840	2,071	15	15	5	10		2,166,540	625,878
New Jersey (a)	25	485		121			216			69	2,251	2,730	735	1,162	835	2,166,540	625,878
New York (a)	14	135									63	739	134	413	172	860,500	262,345
Ohio	1																
Pennsylvania	10	26	7			39	467			27	61	896	256	625	15	1,435,000	366,400
Vermont	1									2	2	13				4,000	2,450

States.	Materials. Raw Silk.	Materials. Silk Yarn.	Materials. Chemicals.	Materials. Other Materials.	Materials. All Materials.	Products. Silk Goods.	Products. Silk Ribbons.	Products. Silk.	Products. Machine Silk.	Products. Spool Silk.	Products. Silk Thread.	Products. Other products.	Products. All products.
The United States	Pounds. 684,438	Pounds. 48,456	Dollars. 389,381	Dollars. 833,736	Dollars. 7,817,539	Yards. 1,093,432	Yards. 3,234,354	Pounds. 370,031	Pounds. 127,560	Pounds. 19,000	Dollars. 3,880,357	Dollars. 12,210,662
Connecticut	175,839		81,614	406,727	2,040,834	636,289	447,664	145,702	36,730		1,396	1,414,130	3,314,845
Maryland													1,402,500
Massachusetts	161,659		46,500	82,900	937,000	109,700	82,860		62,900			1,472,500
New Hampshire	2,000		350	14,350			2,000					25,000
New Jersey	229,787	72,440	43,800	20,555	2,678,161	322,100	1,294,620	55,529	13,400		2,182,784	3,906,904
New York	111,843			24,503	1,211,385		22,000	77,500	7,000		644,573	1,839,073
Ohio												
Pennsylvania	32,425		36,016	308,664	918,681	36,080	1,300,000	6,500	1,000	19,000	1,033,000	1,622,800
Vermont	1,009		200	145	7,805							10,380

a Two establishments, using 3 water-wheels of 4-horse power, employing 62 females and 8 youths, and $12,000 capital, paying $11,030 wages, using $307,014 materials, producing $425,700, included in "Silk, Sewing and Twist," are excluded from this table, as they do not manufacture, but simply wind sewing-silk and twist.

SILK MANUFACTURE IN THE UNITED STATES.

Silk Manufacture, 1880.

States	Number of establishments	Capital	Number of hand-looms on broad goods	Number of hand-looms on narrow goods	Number of power-looms on broad goods	Number of power-looms on narrow goods	Number of spindles winding, cleaning and doubling	Number of spindles spinning and twisting	Number of spindles braiding	Value of machinery	Value of buildings	Greatest number of hands	Average number of hands — Males above 16 years	Average number of hands — Females above 15 years	Average number of hands — Children and youth	Hours in day labor — May to November	Hours in day labor — November to May	Total amount paid in wages during the year
California	5	$164,300		24			209	150	734	62,000	16,400	180	20	106	25	10	10	41,400
Connecticut	28	4,436,500		10	448	155	30,763	53,472		1,247,500	746,000	3,766	785	1,950	633	10	10	1,036,530
Illinois	1	82,000				13				80,000	25,000	404	67	182	57	9½	9½	72,150
Kansas	1	9,500	2	51						1,000	2,500	2	1		1	10	10	230
Maine	1	30,000		89						9,000	3,000	69	9	46	14	11	11	10,150
Maryland	4	50,900		91			228	512		10,000	8,500	82	12	56	14	9	9	11,000
Massachusetts	22	1,300,900	72	2		88	18,514	16,306	11,090	263,950	194,100	2,020	353	1,283	188	10	10	621,735
Missouri	1	4,000								1,000	500	5	3	5	1	10	10	750
New Hampshire	1	8,000		2			350	880		2,000	1,000	19	10	4		10	10	2,300
New Jersey	105	6,862,825	1,444	153	2,017	989	76,687	134,746	33,629	2,290,000	964,100	18,581	4,658	5,369	2,433	10	10	4,171,745
New York	153	4,066,775	85	905	543	552	27,707	89,064	22,784	966,000	1,435,000	10,484	2,405	5,859	1,700	10	10	2,500,025
Ohio	1	24,700		29						12,000	4,000	142	21	78	41	9¾	9¾	12,550
Pennsylvania	49	1,579,900	96	226	95	477	9,495	15,244	6,824	257,000	432,000	3,260	1,000	1,520	319	10	10	678,150
Rhode Island	6	7,500							6,770	5,000	1,000	15		7		10	10	1,100
Vermont	1	2,000					96	326		1,000	500	4		2		10	10	155
Total	382	$19,125,300	1,629	1,524	3,105	2,218	164,318	292,312	81,067	$5,237,500	$3,896,610	34,521	9,575	16,396	5,566			$9,146,702

SILK MANUFACTURE IN THE UNITED STATES.

States.	Value of raw silk and silk materials consumed.	Value of other textile materials consumed.	Value of dye-stuffs, chemicals and oils consumed.	Value of fuel consumed.	Value of all other materials and supplies consumed.	Gross value of materials and supplies; total.	Silk material twice included in foregoing column.	Net value of materials and supplies; total.	Gross value of manufactured products.	Silk products twice included in foregoing column.	Net value of manufactured products, i. e., finished goods.
California	66,418	3,500	8,552	2,855	5,170	80,995	14,995	66,000	150,175	28,470	130,705
Connecticut	3,625,825	12,000	115,040	41,693	117,148	3,911,706	295,190	3,016,516	5,881,000	442,925	5,438,075
Illinois	73,829	9,500	...	...	42,375	125,826	...	125,826	244,150	...	244,150
Kansas	150	...	...	...	...	150	...	150	540	...	540
Maine	50,200	2,290	630	225	1,250	61,395	25,000	36,395	81,683	50,485	31,100
Maryland	11,620	...	1,150	...	15,780	15,780	...	15,780	35,415	...	35,415
Massachusetts	1,753,870	161,915	64,725	15,475	17,330	1,990,515	121,000	1,869,515	3,764,260	273,167	3,491,053
Missouri	580	...	...	...	50	630	...	630	2,500	...	2,500
New Hampshire	11,000	...	300	225	100	11,625	2,750	8,875	15,000	6,300	8,700
New Jersey	8,664,835	63,400	482,473	78,568	369,281	9,678,556	2,506,400	7,108,136	17,198,580	4,971,185	12,251,015
New York	4,359,485	739,550	100,430	24,167	134,192	5,331,804	533,600	4,708,204	10,179,440	862,115	9,358,025
Ohio	14,845	2,075	...	...	2,575	19,495	...	19,495	53,110	...	53,110
Pennsylvania	1,297,705	394,680	30,975	16,265	167,370	1,620,985	494,000	1,426,985	3,491,840	658,675	2,853,165
Rhode Island	7,500	...	...	...	...	7,500	...	7,300	16,000	...	10,000
Vermont	1,140	...	50	20	...	1,210	...	1,210	2,100	...	2,100
Total	$19,928,683	$1,400,480	$803,314	$173,283	$356,941	$22,657,701	$3,898,935	$18,760,166	$41,020,043	$6,513,320	$34,510,723

Quantities of Silk, in products, in 1880.

STATES.	Sewings and twist.	Broad goods and handkerchiefs.	Ribbons and laces.	Trimmings and small goods.
	Pounds.	Yards.	Yards.	Pounds.
Total	821,528	10,856,234	30,129,951	710,149
California	9,500			4,650
Connecticut	394,981	2,253,070	8,541,235	695
Illinois				12,220
Kansas			3,600	
Maine	4,225			
Maryland				1,784
Massachusetts	273,816	99,120	573,320	39,789
Missouri				65
New Hampshire	1,300			300
New Jersey	25,580	6,975,655	8,794,100	50,405
New York	88,765	1,427,439	10,302,696	403,330
Ohio				2,187
Pennsylvania	23,110	101,000	1,915,000	192,824
Rhode Island				1,900
Vermont	251			

Summary of Silk production. Finished goods for the year ending June 30, 1880.

Sewing-silk	$776,120
Machine **twist**	6,007,735
Floss silk	225,025
Dress goods	4,115,205
Satins	1,101,875
Tie silks and scarfs	606,675
Millinery silks	891,955
Other broad **goods**	627,595
Handkerchiefs	3,881,590
Ribbons	6,023,100
Laces	437,000
Braids and bindings	999,685
Fringes and dress trimmings	4,950,275
Cords, tassels, passementerie, and millinery trimmings	1,866,575
Upholstery and military trimmings	1,392,855
Coach laces and carriage trimmings	37,510
Undertakers', hatters', **and fur trimmings**	59,805
Mixed goods and silk values therein	519,643
United States	$34,519,723

SILK MANUFACTURE IN THE UNITED STATES. 59

Silk manufacture in counties producing goods to the value of $1,000,000 *annually.*

State and County.	Number of factories reported.	Capital (real and personal) invested in the business.	Number of looms.	Gross value of manufactured products.	Net value of manufactured products, i. e., value of finished goods.	Total amount paid in wages during the year.
United States.	288	$15,371,575	7,452	$32,906,090	$27,688,170	$7,531,505
CONNECTICUT.						
Hartford county.	3	3,215,000	549	2,709,590	2,571,820	638,760
Tolland county..	9	560,000	37	1,617,145	1,443,060	168,360
MASSACHUSETTS.						
Hampshire c'nty.	4	437,400	......	1,457,300	1,416,600	203,625
NEW JERSEY.						
Hudson county..	17	753,300	1,060	2,045,000	2,028,400	485,560
Passaic county..	82	5,660,525	3,238	14,164,465	10,003,905	3,335,045
NEW YORK.						
New York c'nty.	126	3,431,450	1,799	7,800,250	7,596,720	2,079,535
PENNSYLVANIA.						
Philadel. county	47	1,313,900	769	3,162,340	2,627,665	620,620

In the present census the returns show a total of "capital" amounting to $19,125,300. If the assumption be made that the money used in carrying on the business, apart from plant and fixtures, is turned over three times in the year, the following estimate may be offered:

One-third of $9,146,705, the year's expenditure for wages	$3,048,902
One-third of $22,467,701, the year's cost of materials and supplies	7,489,234
Fixed capital in machinery	5,227,500
Fixed capital in buildings	3,836,600
Estimate for total fixed and floating capital	$19,602,236

Giving a result within 2½ per cent. of the returns.

The number of hands reported as the "average" employed, is usually taken from the pay-roll, and no allowance is made for irregularities and absences. The actual number constantly employed is fully ten per cent. below the reported average. A careful study of the returns on this point has justified this conclusion. The rates of wages paid to different classes of operatives during the year ending June 30, 1881, are given in the following table:

Rate of wages per week to specified operatives.

Designation of operatives.	Sex.	Average rate.	Usual rates.
Raw silk winder	F.	$5 25	$5 00 and 6 00
Raw silk cleaner	F.	3 37	3 00
Raw silk doubler	F.	5 18	5 00 and 5 50
Raw silk spinner	M.	5 57	6 00
Do.	F.	4 87	
Raw silk twister	M.	5 98	6 00
Do.	F.	5 67	6 00
Raw silk reeler	F.	4 50	
Soft silk doubler	F.	4 00	
Soft silk winder	F.	6 35	6 00
Soft silk spooler	F.	4 96	
Soft silk warper	M.	10 71	
Do.	F.	7 62	8 00
Quiller and quill winder	F.	4 09	
Soft silk beamer	M.	12 11	12 00 and 15 00
Do.	F.	7 72	7 00 and 9 00
Soft silk warp twister	M.	13 96	12 00 and 15 00
Hand-loom weaver (a)	M.	14 15	12 00, 15 00, 18 00
Do.	F.	8 44	
Power-loom weaver (a)	M.	11 43	12 00
Do.	F.	7 94	
Lace-machine operator	M.	14 75	
Braid-machine operator	M.	16 00	
Braider	F.	5 41	
Passementerie spinner	M.	17 73	
Do.	F.	12 00	
Fringe-knotter	F.	5 30	
Tassel-maker	F.	5 29	
Finisher	M.	13 50	
Designer (b)	M.	24 71	
Card-cutter (c)	M.	11 68	
Dyer (d)	M.	12 77	12 00 and 15 00
Engineer	M.	12 33	
Machinist	M.	12 40	
Loom-fixer	M.	15 87	
Laborer	M.	8 73	6 00 and 9 00

a. There is a very great difference in the size of looms for different kinds of goods. The highest rates paid to power-loom weavers are paid to those employed on the large looms used in fringe and trimming manufacture.

b. The designer is sometimes also the superintendent.

c. The card-cutter is sometimes also the designer.

d. The chief dyer receives from $20 to $30.

SILK MANUFACTURE IN THE UNITED STATES.

The net value of raw silk and silk materials consumed in manufacture is $15,310,148. The gross value, as given in the returns, consists of the following items :

2,690,482 pounds raw silk, valued at.............................	$13,497,203
Silk material twice included in returns............................	3,898,535
Waste silk, pierced cocoons, and imported organzine, tram, French twist, etc...	1,812,945
Total...	19,208,683

Silk material is "twice included" when, for instance, it appears first as "raw silk," in the returns of a throwster, and secondly as "thrown silk" or "fringe silk," being again reported as raw material in the return of a weaver or fringe-maker. The number of pounds of raw silk accounted for in the returns is 2,690,482, which agrees very fairly with the import of the fiscal year, 2,562,236, the stock on hand being somewhat lighter at the close than at the beginning of the year.

Silk products twice included are deducted from the gross production, leaving a result which it will be noticed exactly agrees with the value of finished goods as given by the returns. The reasons for this deduction are similar to those which apply to the values of raw materials. While the total production, as represented by reports amounting to $41,033,045, covers only a real value of product amounting to $34,519,723, it should be noted that the products of partial manufacture go for the most part to be finished in counties and often in states other than those where they originate. Hence in many cases the gross production of a county or state more nearly represents its industry than would the value of its finished goods. For instance, the gross production of Passaic county, New Jersey, $14,164,465, is much nearer the total value of its industry than $10,003,905, the value of its completed goods, because the greater part of the thrown and fringe silk produced in Paterson, New Jersey, is not made into goods there, but goes elsewhere, chiefly to New York city; and the same is true, to a great extent, of the added value from spooling, winding, dyeing, and refinishing; those processes being largely applied in New Jersey to goods belonging in other states.

The values of the finished goods are given at the selling prices in their chief markets, and without deduction for expenses of selling. No questions were asked or answered in the returns as to such expenses, nor as to profit and loss, freight to market, taxes, interest on capital, and depreciation of materials, goods, buildings, or machinery.

Mr. John E. Atwood, of Stonington, Connecticut, has, by request, contributed a letter on the history of silk machinery, which is herewith subjoined:

STONINGTON, CONNECTICUT, *September* 27, 1881.

About fifty years ago nearly all the silk produced and munufactured in the United States was reeled by hand in a rude manner and spun on hand-wheels, each attendant operating a single spindle only. The substitution of machinery near that time, driven by water or steam power, soon superseded the old methods. Like nearly everything of the kind at that period, the earlier appliances for the manufacture of silk were primitive in character. This industry has been affected by a series of advances of more or less importance, among which may be mentioned the application of the friction-roll for a take-up motion in spinning, the use of the railroad machine for doubling and twisting, the three-cord matcher for doubling and matching; also a matcher and evener combined for doubling, and finally an improved process for stretching the twisted silk, that has superseded most of the previous steps by cheapening and improving the product.

In the meantime many minor advantages have been introduced, while steady progress has been made in style and workmanship, insomuch that the modern plant for silk manufacture would hardly seem to be related to the earlier specimens.

These observations apply more particularly to the silk industry up to a very recent period. Within the last two or three years, however, there has been a marked advance at least in the machinery and appliances for throwing silk. These changes are of a radical type and of such superior merits as to work a complete revolution in their sphere of operations. These last steps in the line of improvement apply to both departments of silk throwing, commencing with a most superior guide system, and include important features in winding, redrawing, doubling, reeling, soft silk winding, spinning, etc. While the machinery is far superior to the former styles, at the same time it costs much less for a plant to turn out a given production.

A brief statement as regards the spinning frame, the most important of the series, may not be out of place here.

This machine, unlike its rivals, is adapted for both the sewing and the weaving departments. It contains the new guide system; it has practical self-balancing spindles that will bear a maximum velocity of 10,000 revolutions per minute, and run much better than the common spindles will at 5,000. The spindles are self-oiling, neat, and waste no oil, and require to be oiled but once in from three to six months. The bands will last much longer on this frame. The machine is a model of neatness and convenience. It can be operated with less expensive labor, has several minor advantages, and has a radically new method for driving the spindles. It is very economical of space, the last edition being only 10 inches from the center of the spindles on opposite sides, while it costs less for spindles than any other.

If we stop to survey the progress made at this point we find that one operative will spin more silk and do it much better than 2,000 could a half century ago; the room occupied would be only about one-four-hundredth part as much, and the cost of the machinery about one-twentieth.

In addition to the foregoing statements concerning the progress in machinery it may be desirable to notice the increased use of power-looms. The following statistics have been compiled from the

INDEX

TO SILK MANUFACTURE IN THE UNITED STATES.

                                                                                        PAGE.

Agriculture, Committee (of Congress) on, reports of........................36, 40
    "the father of"... 6
Aliens not permitted to engage in trade or manufacture........................15
Almshouses, English, to furnish silk culturists................................16
American Institute, of New York...39
    Philosophical Society, of Philadelphia....................................29
    silk worn in England:
        by Charles II...14
        by the princess dowager of Wales......................................18
        by Lord Chesterfield..18
        by Queen Caroline...21
        by Queen Charlotte..30
        by Catharine Macaulay...30
Aspinwall, Dr. Nathaniel, of Connecticut..................................29, 31
Atwood, John E., of Stonington, Connecticut................................... 62
    William, of Connecticut...35
Authors, list of, in the *multicaulis* period.................................39
Bancroft's summary of silk culture in Virginia................................14
Berkeley, Governor, experiments with flax, hemp, and silk.....................14
Bingham, Jesse, of Connecticut..35
Blydenburgh, S., of Albany, New York..39
Boston, William Molineaux's attempts in manufacture at........................32
Bounties on silk culture and mulberry trees authorized:
    by California...63
    by Connecticut..33, 38
    by counties, fairs, and stock companies...................................38
    in Georgia..23
    in Georgia, largest ever paid...26
    by Maine..38
    by Massachusetts..38
    by Massachusetts, largest amount to one claimant..........................38
    by New Jersey...29, 38
    by parliament of Great Britain..19, 26
    by parliament, stopped by Revolutionary War...............................19
    by payments in tobacco..14
    at Savannah, stimulating effect of..27
    by Society of Arts (London)...19, 28
    by Vermont..38
    in Virginia...14

                                                                                    PAGE.
Broad goods and handkerchiefs, yards of, in 1880..........................58
          · production of, in 1880..58
Braids and bindings, production of, in 1880.................................58
Brousse, de la...39
Buell, Judge, of Albany, New York...39
Burlington, New Jersey, silk culture in......................................39
California, production of silkworm eggs and cocoons in......................63
Capital employed in silk manufacture, 1880..................................59
Census returns of silk manufacture, 1850, 1860, 1870..................54, 55
                                        1880........................56, 57, 58
Charleston, act to establish a filature at...................................19
Cheney, Seth W., of Connecticut..35
       Ward, & Bros., of Burlington, New Jersey..............................39
Chidsey, Samuel, of Scipio, New York...35
Children, silk culture suitable to the tenderest age of......................19
China re-reeled silk, efforts to obtain......................................45
Clap, Rev. T., president of Yale College.....................................28
Clark, G. B., of New York..38
Clarke, John, of Philadelphia..39
Clothing, parliament urged to forbid colonial manufacture of.................15
Cobb, Jonathan H., of Massachusetts...............................35, 38, 39
Cochineal insect confused with silkworm.......................................8
Cocoons obtained and shipped at New Orleans..................................63
       price of, in America, in 1621...11
       weight of, required to make a pound of raw silk.......................24
       of the wild (alleged) silkworm in Virginia............................13
       size of, in Virginia..13
Comstock, Franklin G., of Philadelphia.......................................39
Conant, Joseph, of Connecticut...35
Congress, silk culture brought to the attention of...........................35
Connecticut, introduction of silk industry into..............................31
       the chief seat of early silk manufacture..............................32
       legislation to encourage silk culture............................31, 36
Convicts, proposed employment of, in silk culture............................17
Cortes appoints officers to promote silk culture in America...................5
Currency, sewing-silk used for, and its debasement.......................33, 34
Dandolo, Count S...39
Davis, Jonathan..39
Dearborn, General Henry Alex. Scammel..39
Delabigarre, Peter, of New York..39
Delgadillo, Diego, credited with first introduction of silk industry..........5
Dennis, Jonathan, jr...35
Deslongchamps, M...39
Diggs, Governor Edward, essays on silk culture...............................14
Dress goods of silk, dates of starting manufacture of........................43
       production of, in 1880..58, 59
Dresses of silk, the first made in New England...............................31
       frequently made before the Revolution.....................30, 31, 32
       worn by eminent persons abroad..............See *American silk*.

	PAGE.
Du Ponceau, Peter S., of Philadelphia..............................36, 37, 39	
Dyestuffs, chemicals, and oils used in manufacture.........................57	
Ebenezer, Georgia, settlement of...22	
beginnings of silk industry at............................22	
product and export, 1770-'72..............................24	
largest production in the state, at........................27	
Eggs of the silkworm, hatched by carrying in the bosom....................22	
sent from Spain to America 5	
shipment from England at first unsuccessful............ 7	
shipment, second, invoice of........................... 9	
Elizabeth (Queen), gown made for, of silk grass............................11	
Eliot, Rev. Dr. Jared, of Connecticut...................................23, 28	
End of silk industry in Georgia..27	
in Louisiana...20	
in New Spain.. 6	
in South Carolina....................................19	
in Virginia..14	
End of the *Morus multicaulis* speculation..................................41	
Evans, Dr. Cadwallader, of Philadelphia..................................29	
Export of American silk goods to Peru.................................... 6	
raw silk from Georgia............................23, 24, 25	
South Carolina.......................................18	
United States in transit to Europe..................45	
textile machinery from England forbidden........................31	
Eyes or buds of the mulberry sufficient for planting........................41	
Farmers angry at their losses...41	
Fessenden, Thomas G., of Boston..39	
Filature, at Charleston, act to establish..................................19	
at Philadelphia, authorized and opened.........................29	
(second one), by Du Ponceau........................37	
at Savannah, built in 1744................................23	
burned in 1757 (afterward rebuilt)..............25	
discontinued and broken up..............*note to*......24	
Fines for neglecting silk culture...14	
Fisher, Grace, of Pennsylvania..30	
Fisk, William A., of Connecticut..35	
Flags of American silk...37	
Floss silk, production of, in 1880.......................................58	
France, measures taken to encourage silk industry in...................... 6	
Franklin, Dr. Benjamin, urges promotion of silk industry....................29	
French Revolution indirectly checks American silk culture..................32	
settlers in Georgia produce and supply sewing silk..............27	
Fuel consumed in manufacture, 1880.....................................57	
Garden, public, at Savannah......................... 21	
Gates, Sir Thomas, testimony as to growth of mulberry trees 8	
Gee, Joshua, estimate of comparative value of negro labor..................16	
George II directs a silver seal to be made for Georgia.....................26	
Georgia and South Carolina denominated "silk colonies"...................26	
historical error as to export of raw silk from.............24, 25	

	PAGE.
Georgia, introduction of silk industry into	20
separated from the Carolinas	20
trustees of, favor the cultivation of silk and wine	20
Handkerchiefs, silk, Centennial exhibition promotes manufacture of	44
dates of starting manufacture of	43, 44
production of, in 1880	58
Hanks, Rodney and Horatio, of Connecticut	35
William, of Mansfield, Connecticut	32
Hartlib, Samuel, essay of, on the reformed Virginia silkworm	12
Hazzi, Count von, of Munich, Bavaria	36, 39
Henry IV, of France, encourages the silk industry	7
Homergue, John d, of Philadelphia	30, 35, 36, 39
Horstmann, William H., of Philadelphia	34
Hovey, Storrs, of Connecticut	35
Hughes, John, of Pennsylvania	28
Huguenots introduce silk industry into South Carolina	15
Imports of raw silk	46, 47
silk manufactures	49, 53
in fiscal years 1825–'80	48
in calendar years 1851–'80	48
specifying articles, 1871–'80	49
Indians to be taught silk culture	13
Ingersoll, Jared, of Connecticut	28
Instructions for silk culture, book of, sent by James I	10, 11
Introduction of the mulberry tree into America	5
silkworm into America	5
silk industry into Georgia	20
Louisiana	19
Pennsylvania	28
South Carolina	15
Inventions: improvements in machinery during fifty years	62
reels, improved	35
reeling from cocoons and making sewing-silk at once	42
reeling, doubling, and twisting at once	42
spinning-wheel improved by double wheel head	34
throwing and twisting, improved machine for	31
water-power machinery in Connecticut	35
Iron and steel manufacture forbidden in the colonies	31
Italians brought to Georgia to teach silk culture	22
Jacquard attachments in use in silk manufacture, 1880	63
James I, of England, encourages the silk industry at home	7
sends silkworm eggs to Virginia	7, 9
quarrels with the Virginia Company	11
Japan, raw silk from, excellence of	45
Johnson, Sir Nathaniel, efforts in silk culture	16
Kansas, production of raw silk in 1880	64
Kenrick, William	39
King Charles II wears American silk	14

	PAGE.
Laces, silk, manufacture of, at Ipswich, Massachusetts	34
dates of starting	43, 44
production of, in 1880	58
Land grant for mulberry planting at **Greenbush, New York**	38
value per acre when planted with mulberry trees	40, 41
Lardner, Dr. Dionysius	39
Law, Governor, wears garments of New England silk	31
Law, John, speculative schemes of	19
Lilly, Alfred, of Connecticut	35
Logan, James, recommends the industry to the **Penn family**	27
Lombe, Sir Thomas, opinion on silk industry	20
great silk-throwing mill in England	17
weaves a dress of American silk	21
Looms, hand and power, numbers of, in 1880	56
power, increase in numbers of, 1875–'80	63
Louisiana, introduction of silk industry into	19
Machinery in use in 1837 for silk manufacture	42
value of, in silk manufacture, 1880	56
improvements in....See *Inventions*.	
Machines used in silk manufacture, number of, in 1880	63
Mansfield, **Connecticut**, early seat of silk industry	31
production of, per year	33, 35
Mantua, piece of, woven from home-grown cocoons	30
Manufactures in America, measures to prevent	15, 28, 30, 31
committee (of Congress) on, report of	36
of silk, in America, the earliest	6
dates of starting of different kinds of	43, 44
in different localities	43
in Connecticut, a household art	32, 33
in England	15, 16, 17
imports of, by chart	52
in Massachusetts before the Revolution	32
in 1837	42
in 1855	46
in South Carolina, mixed fabrics	16
in Virginia, attempted	15
Manufactures of silk in the United States in 1880:	
in counties producing $1,000,000 per year	59
in pounds and yards produced	58
proportion of home product to consumption	50
production, by chart	52
of finished goods, 1874–'80	51
gross	57
net	57
net and gross, remarks on	61
summary of	58
some are twice included in returns	61
statistics of, 1844, 1850, 1855	46
1850, 1860, 1870	54, 55
1880	56, 57, 58

	PAGE.
Manufacturers of silk involved in the *multicaulis* speculation	41
Marshall, John, appropriation for the encouragement of	31
Massachusetts, silk manufacture in	32, 34, 42, 46
Mease, James, M. D., of Philadelphia	39
Millinery silks, production of, in 1880	58
Mills, silk, earliest, at Mansfield, Connecticut	35
and factories, number of, in 1880	56
Mississippi Company organized by John Law	19
silk-culture on the banks of the	19
Mixed silk fabrics, earliest manufacture of, in America	16
and silk values therein, 1880	58
Molineaux, William, starts silk manufacture at Boston	32
Morin, M.	39
Morris, Edmund, of Burlington, New Jersey	39
Morus alba, speculative prices for	42
Morus multicaulis mania, 1830–'41	37, 41
period, literature of	39
Motto of colonial seal of Georgia	20
silver seal of Georgia	26
Mulberry trees in America, introduction of	5
at Burlington, New Jersey, number of, sold	40
in Chelsea Park, London	note to 19
in Connecticut, the planting of	31
in England, 10,000 to each county	7
in France, brought from Italy	6
in Georgia, estimate of number	23
their planting compulsory	20
gifts of, by Dr. Nathaniel Aspinwall	29
land grant for planting	38
Morus multicaulis first introduced	37
near New Orleans, the planting of	20
in New Spain, the planting of	5
in Oatland royal gardens, England	7
prices of, during period of speculation	40, 42
at Savannah, in the trustees' garden	21
in South Carolina, flourishing	18
and sugar-beet culture, recommended	37
in Virginia, their planting compulsory	10
abundance of	8
National silk convention	38
Navigation laws, British, effect on silk industry	15
Negro labor proposed for silk culture	16
women, want of, checks silk industry	19
Nets, silk, date of starting manufacture of	44
New England, first garments of home-grown silk in	31
New Jersey legislature, bounties offered by	29, 38
New Spain, silk introduced into	5
Oglethorpe, General, takes Georgia silk to England	21
Oatlands, England, mulberry trees in royal gardens at	7

INDEX TO SILK MANUFACTURE IN THE UNITED STATES. 71

	PAGE.
Operatives, numbers of, 1880	56, 59
Ortolengi, M., superintendent of filature at Savannah	28
Palmetto leaves not used by silkworms	8
Pascalis, Dr. Felix, of New York	37, 39
Paupers, employment of, in silk manufacture at Boston	32
proposition to employ, in silk culture	16
Penn family, the silk industry recommended to	27
Pennsylvania, introduction of silk industry	27
ladies wear silk of their own raising	30
Perrottet, Samuel, of Paris	37
Philadelphia, establishment of first filature	29
second filature	37
mulberry trees planted near	29
Pinckney, Mrs., takes American silk to England	18
Pollock, Cullen, of North Carolina	28
George, of North Carolina	28
Pongees, the printing of	44
Premiums for silk and mulberry culture...See *Bounties*.	
Prices of mulberry trees (speculative)	40, 42
silk goods in successive years	43
Profit and loss, no account of, in census returns	61
Pullein, Samuel	39
Punishments for neglecting silk culture	14
Purry, John Peter, brings Swiss colonists to South Carolina	18
Quality of American-grown silk, testimony of Charles II	14
Sir Thomas Lombe	18
Quantities of silk (pounds and yards) made in 1880	58
Queen Caroline wears American silk	21
Charlotte wears American silk	30
Elizabeth wears American "silk grass"	11
Raw materials of manufacture, alleged loss by importing	17
textile, other than silk	57
sometimes twice reported	61
Raw silk in America, earliest quotation of prices of	11
from Asia, beginning of importation	45
into England, imports of, from Italy	16, 21, 23
admitted duty free from colonies	26
in Georgia, production of	24
historical error in export of	25
imports of, 1831-'36; 1843-'80	46, 47
reeling of, the need of good	45
from South Carolina, exports of	18
product since *multicaulis* speculation	63
and silk materials consumed in manufacture	57
twice included in returns	61
weight of cocoons to furnish a pound of	24
Raynal, Abbe, reasons of, for failure of silk culture	19
Reeling China silk, efforts for improving	45

	PAGE.
Reeling in Connecticut, primitive methods	33
bounties for proficiency in	23
at Ebenezer, Georgia	22
implements for, distributed in Georgia	23
improvements in machinery for	35
instructor in, sent to Georgia	21
Italian proficients in, sent to Georgia	22
Revolutionary War, effect of, on silk industry	30, 32
Ribbons and laces (silk), yards of, in 1880	58
(silk), dates of starting manufacture	44
production of, in 1880	58
Rixford, Nathan, of Connecticut	35
Roberts, E. P., of Baltimore	39
Ruffin, Edmund, of Richmond, Virginia	39
Rush, Richard, Secretary of the Treasury, report to	36, 39
Rutherford, John, of North Carolina	28
Salza (Bavaria), emigration from the valley of	22
Satins, date of starting manufacture of	44
production of, in 1880	58
Savannah, establishment of filature at	23
filature discontinued at	note to 24
Seal, colonial, of Georgia, representing silkworms	20
of silver, for Georgia, representing a tender of silk	26
Selling expenses not called for in census returns	61
Serres, Oliver de, of France	6
Sewing-silk and twist, pounds produced in 1880	58
dates of starting manufacture of	43
early history of manufacture of	32
length of skein defined by legislation	34
manufacture of, 1844 and 1850	46
production of, in 1880	58
as a substitute for money, in currency	34
Silk culture as an expedient to prevent manufacture	28
Silk grass, a gown of, made for Queen Elizabeth	11
Silk Hope plantation, in South Carolina	16, 18
Silkworm alleged to be found wild in America	8, 12
in palmetto leaves	8
eggs, the first in America	5
subsequent shipments	7, 9
Skinner, John S.	39
Slavery in the colonies encouraged by James I.	9
Smith, Gideon B., of Baltimore	35, 39
Snow, Eliphalet	35
Society of Arts, London, bounties for silk culture	19
South Carolina, introduction of the industry into	15
and Georgia denominated silk colonies	26
silk products of, credited to Georgia	18
South Sea bubble	19

	PAGE.
Spindles, numbers of, in 1880	56
Spun silk, date of starting manufacture	44
Stiles, Dr. **Ezra, President** of Yale College	31
Sully insults **the silk merchants of Paris**	6
Summers, Sir George, **expedition of, with a fleet of vessels**	7
Swiss silk-culturists in **South Carolina**	18
Taffeta, the first made in America	6
Tapestry, silk, date of starting manufacture of	45
Throwing silk, Sir Thomas Lombe's great mill for	17
Thrown silk, estimate of import of, into Great Britain	21
Throwsters, silk, company of, chartered in 1629	11
journeymen, emigrating to America	28
Tie silks and scarfs, production of, **in** 1880	58
Tinelli, Signor	39
Tobacco, bounties payable in	14
more profitable than **silk**	15
proclamation against, by **James I**	9
uprooted in **Great** Britain	9
Trimmings and small goods, pounds **of, in** 1880	58
silk, beginnings of manufacture of	34, 42
dates of starting **manufacture of**	34, 42, 44
production of, in 1880	58
United Society for Promoting **American Manufactures**	31
Utah, production of **raw** silk in, **1880**	64
Velvet manufacture **still an experiment**	45
Vernon, W. H.	40
Virginia, introduction of silk industry into	8
Wages paid to operatives **in 1880**	56
rates of, per week, to specified **operatives**	60
Water-power machinery for silk-throwing in England	17
used in silk manufacture, early attempts	35
Weaving broad silks in England begun about **1620**	11
Whitmarsh, Samuel, of Northampton	39, 41
Williams, E. W., essays on silk culture	12
Windham and Tolland counties, Connecticut, memorial from	36
Women, silk culture suitable to the weakness of their sex	19
Wright, Susannah, of Columbia, Pennsylvania	30

TENTH

Annual Report

OF THE

Silk Association

OF AMERICA.

WEDNESDAY, MAY 16th, 1882.

TABLE OF CONTENTS,

OF THE

TENTH ANNUAL REPORT

OF THE

SILK ASSOCIATION OF AMERICA.

Officers of the Association, 1882-1883.........................77
Members of the Association May 16th, 1882....................79
Secretary's Report,...83
Statistics,...91
Silk Manufactures; Production in 1881,........................93
Imports of Raw Silk in Calendar Years,........................94
Imports of Raw Silk in Fiscal Years,..........................95
Imports of Raw Silk by Countries,.............................96
Imports of Raw Silk at New York and San Francisco, separate,..97
Imports of Waste Silk and Cocoons,............................97
Imports of Silk Manufactures in Calendar Years,...............98
Imports of Silk Manufactures in Fiscal Years,.................99
Imports of Silk Manufactures by Months,......................100
Sugar, Molasses, etc., Duties in Detail,.....................101
Wool, and Woolen Manufactures, Duties in Detail,.............101
Silk Manufactures, Duties in Detail,.........................102
Cotton Manufactures, Duties in Detail,.......................103
Duty Paying Imports of the United States,....................104

THE SILK ASSOCIATION OF AMERICA.

OFFICERS, 1882-1883.

President.

FRANK W. CHENEY,............... Hartford, Conn.

Vice-Presidents.

B. RICHARDSON,.................. New York.
C. LAMBERT,...................... Paterson, N. J.
A. B. STRANGE,................... New York.

Treasurer.

LOUIS FRANKE,................... New York.

Directors.

F. O. HORSTMANN,............... Philadelphia, Pa.
IRA DIMOCK,..................... Hartford, Conn.
WM. STRANGE,.................... Paterson, N. J.
JOHN N. STEARNS,................ New York.
WILLIAM SKINNER,................ Holyoke, Mass.
S. E. HUNTINGTON,............... New York.
GEORGE H. BURRITT,.............   "
L. BAYARD SMITH,................   "
MILO M. BELDING,................   "
A. G. JENNINGS,................. Brooklyn, N. Y.
S. W. CLAPP,.................... New York.
WM. T. RYLE,....................   "
JOHN T. WALKER,.................   "
JOHN D. CUTTER,................. Newark, N. J.
HERMAN SIMON,................... Town of Union, N. J.
S. M. MEYENBERG,................ Hoboken, N. J.
JAMES BOOTH,.................... Paterson, N. J.
ALBERT TILT,....................   "   "
J. SILBERMANN,.................. New York.
JOSEPH LOTH,....................   "

Secretary.

WM. C. WYCKOFF,................. 446 Broome Street, N. Y.

LIST OF MEMBERS

OF

THE SILK ASSOCIATION OF AMERICA.

May 16th, 1882.

Adachi, Nanishiro,................7 Warren Street, New York.
Arai, R.,........................18 Mercer Street,   "
Armstrong, Benjamin A.,..........................New London, Conn.
Arnold, Frank,..............477–481 Broome Street, New York.
Atwood, Eugene,................................Stonington, Conn.
Aub, Hackenburg & Co.,.......................Philadelphia, Pa.
Auffmordt, C. A. & Co.,..........33–35 Greene Street, New York.
Banning, David L.,..............87 Leonard Street,   "
Belding, A. N.,...............................Rockville, Conn.
Belding, D. W.,................................Cincinnati, Ohio.
Belding, H. H.,..................................Chicago, Ill.
Belding, Milo M.,..................456 Broadway, New York.
Blydenburgh, Jesse S.,..............66 Pine Street,   "
Boettger, Henry W.,................47 Mercer Street,   "
Boissiére, E. V. de,........Williamsburgh, Franklin Co., Kansas.
Booth, James,...................................Paterson, N. J.
Booth, J. H. & Co.,..............54 Howard Street, New York.
Bottum, C. L.,..............................Northampton, Mass.
Bowman, John A.,..................................Boston,   "
Bridge, Frederick,.................32 Burling Slip, New York.
Brown, L. D. & Son,........................Middletown, Conn.
Brown, Wm. P.,..........457–463 W. 45th Street, New York.
Burritt, George H.,.................32 Burling Slip,   "
Busch, Peter,....................108 Grand Street,   "
Butler, H. V.,...................32 Reade Street,   "

Chaffanjon, Claude,................... Jersey City Heights, N. J.
Chaffee, O. S. & Son,.................. Mansfield Centre, Conn.
Chapin, J. L.,....................... 96 Reade Street, New York.
Cheney, Frank W.,.................... South Manchester, Conn.
Cheney, Harry G.,....................   "   "   "
Cheney, Knight D.,...................   "   "   "
Cheney, James W.,....................   "   "   "
Cheney, John S.,.....................   "   "   "
Cheney, Richard O.,..................   "   "   "
Clapp, S. W.,....................... 7 Mercer Street, New York.
Comby, John,........................... West Hoboken, N. J.
Copcutt, Wm. H. & Co.,....................... Yonkers, N. Y.
Cutter, John D.,.............................. Newark, N. J.
Dimock, Ira,................................ Hartford, Conn.
Dunlop, John,............................... Paterson, N. J
Eaton, E. W.,..................... 19 Mercer Street, New York.
Eldridge, Henry,..................... 435 Broadway,   "
Erskine, James M.,................ 52 Greene Street,   "
Fogg, Wm. H.,..................... 32 Burling Slip,   "
Franke, Louis,................................ Paterson, N. J.
Fukui, M.,.. Japan.
Funke, Hugo,,..................... College Point, L. I., N. Y.
Gibbes, A. H.,....................... 93 Wall Street, New York.
Grimshaw, John,.............................. Paterson, N. J.
Griswold Worsted Co.,........................ Philadelphia, Pa.
Hadden & Co.,................. 109–111 Worth Street, New York.
Hayden, J. H. & Son,..................... Windsor Locks, Conn.
Hayes, Thomas F.,................. 5–9 Union Square, New York.
Hill, A. G.,............................... Florence, Mass.
Horstmann, F. O.,........................... Philadelphia, Pa.
Huntington, S. E.,.................... 31 Burling Slip, New York.
Itschner, W. & Co., ... Philadelphia, Pa.
Jennings, A. G.,............................. Brooklyn, N. Y.
Jennings, W. P.,.............. 473–475 Broome Street, New York.
Johnson, Rowland,................. 54 Beaver Street, New York.
Jourdeuil & Pinckney,..................... West Hoboken, N. J.
Kai, Oria,........................ 30 Howard Street, New York.

Lambert, C., ... Paterson, N. J.
Lathrop Bros., ... Northampton, Mass.
Loewenstine, J. H., ... 187 Church Street, New York.
Loth, Joseph, ... 458 Broome Street, "
Low, A. A., ... 31 Burling Slip, "
Low, A. Augustus, ... 31 " " "
Low, Seth, ... 31 " " "
Ludwig, E., ... 454 Broome Street, "
Lyman, Joseph, ... 31 Burling Slip, "
Meyenberg, S. M., ... Hoboken, N. J.
Milton, Wm. F., ... 159 Maiden Lane, New York.
Morgenroth, Gustavus A., Jr., ... 159 " " "
Morlot, George, ... Paterson, N. J.
Murray, Russell, ... 52 Greene Street, New York.
Muzard, L., ... 13 Mercer Street, "
O'Donoghue, D., ... 91 Grand Street, "
Paul, Frank, ... Montreal, Canada.
Pelgram & Meyer, ... Paterson, N. J.
Plunkett, Thos. F., ... Hartford, Conn.
Pomeroy, S. W., Jr., ... 59 Wall Street, New York.
Richardson, B., ... 5 Mercer Street, "
Richardson, Frank G., ... 5 Mercer Street, "
Rossmässler, Richard, ... Philadelphia, Pa.
Ryle, John C., ... Paterson, N. J.
Ryle, William T., ... 54 Howard Street, New York.
Seavey, J. W. C., ... Canton, Mass.
Silbermann, J. & Co., ... 35 Mercer Street, New York.
Simes, Charles F., ... 46 Howard Street, "
Simon, Herman, ... Town of Union, N. J.
Simon, Robert, ... " " "
Simonds, J. H., ... Warehouse Point, Conn.
Skinner, George B. & Co., ... Yonkers, N. Y.
Skinner, William, ... Holyoke, Mass.
Skinner, William C., ... 43 Mercer Street, New York.
Smith, Benjamin D., ... 113 Water Street, "
Smith, L. Bayard, ... 77 William Street, "
Smith, L. O., ... Philadelphia, Pa.

Smith, S. K., ... Pittsfield, Mass.
Stearns, Henry K., ... 458 Broome Street, New York.
Stearns, John N., ... 458   "   "   "   .
Stelle, Louis R., ... Sauquoit (near Utica) N. Y.
Stevens, E. W., ... 130 Water Street, New York.
Strange, A. B., ... 96-98 Prince Street,   "
Strange, Theodore A., ... 96-98   "   "   "
Strange, William, ... Paterson, N. J.
Streuli, Alfred, ... 70 Mercer Street, New York
Struss, Henry W., ... 110 Grand Street,   "
Takahashi, S. K., (Consul of Japan) 7 Warren Street,   "
Tilt, Albert, ... Paterson, N. J.
Walker, John T., ... 81 Pine Street, New York.
Walter, Richard, ... 452-458 W. 46th Street,   "   "
Warner, Luther J., ... Northampton, Mass.
Westervelt, E., ... 42 Cedar Street, New York.
Wetmore, Cryder & Co., ... 73-74 South Street,   "
Wilson, H. B., ... 33-35 Greene Street,   "
Yamao, K., ... 24-26 Murray Street,   "

HONORARY MEMBERS.

Allen, Franklin, ... Brooklyn, N. Y.
Haywood, George M., ... 39 White Street, New York.
Mackay, J. P., Secretary, ... Paterson, N. J.
Ryle, John, ...   "   "
Takaki, Samro, ... Yokohama, Japan.
Tomita, Tetsnoski, ... London, Eng.

Secretary's Report.

In conformity with the by-laws of the Association, the Secretary has the honor to submit the following report, prepared under direction of the Board of Government, and presenting a review for the past year of the transactions of the Silk Association of America.

The most important event of the past year to the manufacturers of the United States is the adoption of a measure by Congress which gives promise of an intelligent investigation of the tariff by a commission. The debates in Congress which preceded the passage of this bill, brought out in striking relief the wide variety of opinions held on tariff subjects by our legislators. Their knowledge on these subjects was also shown to be strikingly diverse in amount and worth. If there had not been during the whole debate, a firm hope of the final passage of the bill, many of the speeches would have excited grave anxiety among our manufacturers, because of the ignorance displayed respecting industrial interests by some of the speakers, and the bitterness of their opposition to a protective tariff. Great credit is due to those members of Congress who met such opponents with invincible arguments and facts. The thanks of the silk manufacturers are especially due to Congressman John Hill of New Jersey for his able presentation of the growth of the silk industry, bringing together its statistics and showing in sharp light the contrast between the condition of its operatives here and in Europe.

Because of the general hope that the tariff commission bill would pass, there was no disturbance of business such as is usual during the winter months when Congress is in session and the tariff is under debate. Manufacturers have had, however, quite sufficient excitement in the necessity for meeting sharp competition in business, both from abroad and at home.

The imports of European silk goods have been larger than in any preceding twelve months except the year ending June 30th 1872, and will closely approach that extraordinary amount.

Although the year has not been marked by wide variations in the prices of raw silk, there have been important changes in the character of the supply. Rumors of a short crop both in Europe and Asia produced a temporary rise in price late in the Spring of 1881, which was maintained only until the facts of supply became more definitely known. The advance of prices had the most marked effect in Japan, where it laid the basis for an extensive speculation.

Holding for the most part their costly purchases for still higher prices, the Japanese realized little profit from the rise. While the market was readjusting itself in the prospect of a decline they most unwisely attempted a combination to control the delivery to foreigners. This was met on the part of the foreign houses by an agreement not to purchase under the proposed restrictions. During the dispute the raw silk trade of Japan remained stagnant, and exports were almost wholly confined to Japanese houses. This condition of affairs lasted through the greater part of the Autumn months, until a compromise was effected between the contending parties.

The interference of the Japanese combination, by preventing foreigners from their usual purchases, undoubtedly gave an impulse toward the use of European raw silks by our manufacturers. This tendency was greatly strengthened by the demand for a better class of goods in this market, and by a marked deterioration in the quality of Japanese raw silk. The so-called "filature Japans" received during the past year were inferior to anything of the kind since silks of that designation have been in use in this country. Complaints were loud, and with good reason. Many of these silks have been poor in quality, irregular in size, and mixed in color. The resulting "loss

RATES OF WAGES IN SILK MANUFACTURE PER WEEK, IN DOLLARS.

Designation of operative.	Sex.	Average per United States census 1879–1880.	Recent in United States (1882).	Estimated average in England.*	Estimated average in Germany.	Estimated average in France.	Estimated average in Italy.
Hard silk winder*	F.	$5.25	.....	$2.96	.....	$1.40	.....
Hard silk doubler	F.	5.18	.....	.....	.....	2.45	.....
Hard silk spinner	M.	5.57	.....	.....	.....	.....	$2.10
Do	F.	4.87	$5.00	.....	.....	2.00	1.44
Hard silk twister	M.	5.98	.....	.....	.....	3.42	.....
Do	F.	5.67	.....	.....	.....	2.10	.....
Soft silk winder	F.	6.35	8.00	.....	.....	2.00	.....
Warper	M.	10.71	.....	.....	.....	.....	.....
Do	F.	7.62	10.00	.....	.....	2.40	.....
Beamer†	M.	12.11	.....	.....	.....	.....	.....
Do†	F.	7.72	.....	.....	.....	.....	.....
Warp twister	M.	13.96	.....	.....	.....	.....	.....
Weaver on hand-looms‡	M.	14.15	.....	.....	$3.93	5.40	4.80
Do	F.	8.44	.....	.....	2.72	3.00	2.28
Weaver on power-looms	M.	11.43	.....	5.40	3.00	.....	.....
Do	F.	7.94	.....	4.38	.....	.....	.....
Weaver of plain common ribbons	.....	.....	.....	.....	.....	2.70	.....
Weaver of better grade ribbons	.....	.....	.....	.....	.....	3.90	.....
Weaver of fancy ribbons	.....	.....	.....	.....	.....	5.10	.....
Weaver of best novelty ribbons	.....	.....	15.00	.....	.....	9.60	.....
Weaver of damasks	M.	.....	.....	.....	3.93	.....	.....
Weaver of dress-goods	M.	.....	12.00	.....	2.73	6.00	.....
Do	F.	.....	9.00	.....	1.66	.....	.....
Weaver of plush, &c	M.	.....	.....	.....	4.07	.....	.....
Do	F.	.....	.....	.....	2.76	.....	.....
Loom fixer†	M.	15.87	.....	.....	.....	.....	.....
Finisher †	M.	13.50	.....	.....	.....	.....	.....
Designer	M.	24.71	.....	12.00	.....	.....	.....
Lace operative (machine)	M.	14.75	15.00	9.11	.....	.....	.....
Do	F.	5.00	.....	3.00	1.00	3.60	.....
Braid operative (machine)§	M.	16.00	.....	.....	7.90	.....	.....
Braider§	F.	5.41	.....	.....	2.32	.....	.....
Fringe-maker	F.	5.30	.....	.....	1.43	.....	.....
Dyer	M.	12.77	.....	7.00	.....	.....	3.30

*Lower figures are given for wages of children in England.
†Not separately employed under such designations in Europe.
‡Hand-looms are more used than power-looms in Europe; the reverse is true here. Statistics from Europe do not distinguish the two classes.
§Systems of employment here and in Europe differ materially.

The Secretary has the pleasure of announcing the publication of his Report on the Silk Manufactures of the United States, for the United States Census of 1880. The number of copies issued by the Government Printing Office is, however, unexpectedly limited. He takes this opportunity to express his thanks to the members of the Association and to silk manufacturers in general, for the completeness of their returns to the census inquiries of 1880.

The removal of the office of the Association to 446 Broome St., is also a subject for congratulation, as the new premises are well adapted for the uses of the Association, and will in all respects be found more agreeable and convenient than the former quarters.

The sorrowful duty devolves upon the Secretary to record the death of six members of the Association during the past year, as follows:

> WILLIAM RYLE, of New York.
>
> ETHELBERT M. LOW, of NEW YORK.
>
> WM. A. GRISWOLD, of Philadelphia.
>
> J. JACKSON SCOTT, of Paterson.
>
> J. FETTIS, of New York.
>
> S. SHIMURA, of New York.

At a meeting of the Association November 10th 1881, the following resolutions were adopted.

IN THE PROVIDENCE OF GOD, death has removed from us our friend and associate, MR. WILLIAM RYLE, who was one of the founders of this Association, and has been ever since, and was at the time of his death, a Vice-President thereof.

Throughout the entire existence of the Association, MR. RYLE has taken a deep interest in its welfare, giving it liberal and hearty support, and the benefit of his valuable advice and counsel. He was identified with the Silk Industry of this country, and took a personal interest in a project for a School of Design and Technical Education, intended to benefit the working classes and the silk manufacture in general; he was eminent as a merchant of unblemished honor and integrity, and of high public spirit.

By the death of MR. RYLE, the Silk Association of America has lost a faithful and efficient Vice-President, a wise counsellor and a trusted friend.

The sincere sympathies of the Silk Association of America are hereby tendered to the family of MR. RYLE.

The foregoing report was read accepted and ordered to be printed, at the annual meeting of the Silk Association of America, held at 446 Broome Street, May 16th, 1882; and this action was further confirmed at a meeting of the Board of Government held at a subsequent date after the report was in type.

WM. C. WYCKOFF,

Secretary.

Silk Manufacture

IN THE UNITED STATES.

PRODUCTION OF FINISHED GOODS,

In the Calendar Year ending December 31st, 1881.

Sewing-silk, Machine Twist &c.,	$7,689,512
Dress and Piece Goods,	6,832,929
Tie Silks and Scarfs,	584,666
Millinery Silks,	902,592
Handkerchiefs,	5,012,007
Ribbons,	6,213,804
Laces,	450,323
Braids and Bindings,	1,142,454
Trimmings &c.,	6,399,450
Mixed Goods &c.,	729,985
TOTAL,	35,957,722

RECAPITULATION.

Sewings, Twist and Floss Silk,	$ 7,689,512
Broad Goods,	8,320,187
Handkerchiefs, Ribbons and Laces,	11,676,134
Trimmings and Small Goods,	7,541,904
Mixed Goods and Silk values therein,	729,985
TOTAL,	35,957,722

IMPORTS OF RAW SILK AT NEW YORK AND SAN FRANCISCO,
IN THE CALENDAR YEARS.

MONTHS.	1881. Bales.	1881. Value.	1880. Bales.	1880. Value.	1879. Bales.	1879. Value.	1878. Bales.	1878. Value.	1877. Bales.	1877. Value.	1876. Bales.	1876. Value.
July,	1,948	$1,031,400	1,798	$1,026,190	153	$102,124	804	$424,932	974	$666,506	1,555	$628,131
August,	1,644	837,823	2,147	1,177,542	2,493	1,203,467	959	497,737	1,281	818,844	1,162	479,856
September,	2,080	1,142,204	2,737	1,393,635	1,358	727,885	1,177	634,944	1,342	879,466	1,272	521,859
October,	1,716	938,512	897	532,404	1,333	706,697	999	515,329	339	222,214	568	258,641
November,	1,445	706,916	1,951	1,075,375	908	465,839	1,034	407,643	988	499,609	900	347,559
December,	1,437	718,651	1,441	763,920	1,921	934,443	968	438,831	846	480,599	966	403,419
January,	1,171	610,609	957	472,827	894	497,614	515	258,485	224	137,989	142	54,072
February,	967	529,978	649	360,043	1,274	640,342	627	287,174	692	327,013	195	85,541
March,	2,141	1,182,135	2,391	1,352,478	1,521	791,138	1,276	663,207	905	470,576	1,323	651,194
April,	1,177	737,238	2,242	1,280,170	2,155	1,137,293	1,733	893,685	797	355,100	743	484,616
May,	3,859	2,131,334	1,234	732,364	1,239	725,183	1,933	998,248	395	199,490	985	701,643
June,	2,107	1,370,065	2,455	1,311,779	3,687	1,989,307	1,699	839,427	1,236	592,849	1,482	1,009,758
TOTALS,	21,692	11,936,865	20,899	11,478,727	18,936	9,921,332	13,724	6,859,692	10,019	5,650,255	11,293	5,626,299

Compiled by the Secretary of the Silk Association of America, 446 Broome Street, New York.

IMPORTS OF RAW SILK AT THE PORTS OF NEW YORK AND SAN FRANCISCO,

IN FISCAL YEARS ENDING JUNE 30TH.

Months.	1881–1882.		1880–1881.		1879–1880.		1878–1879.		1877–1878.		1876–1877.	
	Bales.	Value.	Bales.	Value.	Bales.	Value.	Bales.	Value.	Bales.	Value.	Bales.	Value.
July,	1,171	$610,609	957	$472,827	894	$497,614	515	$258,485	224	$137,989	142	$54,072
August,	967	529,978	649	360,043	1,274	640,342	627	287,174	692	327,013	195	85,541
September,	2,141	1,182,135	2,391	1,352,478	1,521	791,138	1,276	663,207	905	470,576	1,323	651,194
October,	1,177	737,238	2,242	1,280,170	2,155	1,137,293	1,733	893,685	797	355,100	743	484,616
November,	3,859	2,131,334	1,234	732,364	1,239	725,183	1,933	998,248	395	199,490	985	701,643
December,	2,107	1,370,065	2,455	1,311,779	3,687	1,989,307	1,699	839,427	1,236	592,849	1,482	1,009,758
January,	1,582	974,471	1,948	1,031,400	1,798	1,026,190	153	102,124	804	424,982	974	666,506
February,	1,756	1,115,482	1,644	837,823	2,147	1,177,542	2,493	1,203,467	959	497,737	1,281	818,844
March,	1,712	1,083,017	2,080	1,142,204	2,737	1,393,635	1,358	727,885	1,177	634,944	1,342	879,466
April,	2,165	1,422,861	1,716	938,512	897	532,404	1,333	706,697	999	515,329	339	222,214
May,	1,711	1,158,570	1,445	706,916	1,951	1,075,375	908	465,839	1,034	407,643	988	499,609
June,	1,334	862,138	1,437	718,651	1,441	763,920	1,921	934,443	968	438,831	846	480,599
Totals,	21,682	13,177,898	20,198	10,885,167	21,741	11,749,943	15,949	8,080,681	10,190	5,002,483	10,640	6,554,062

Compiled by the Secretary of the Silk Association of America, 446 Broome Street, New York.

IMPORTS OF RAW SILK AT NEW YORK AND SAN FRANCISCO,
CLASSIFIED BY COUNTRIES OF EXPORT:
For the Fiscal Year ending June 30th, 1882.

MONTHS.	Shipments from Europe.				Shipments from Asia.						TOTAL.	
	Strictly European.		Reshipped Asiatic.		Japan.		Hong Kong.		Shanghai.			
	Bales.	Value.	Bales.	Value.	Bales.	Value.	Bales.	Value.	Bales.	Value.	Bales.	Value.
July, 1881	34	$44,370	220	$13,583	299	$187,520	63	$22,711	555	$242,425	1,171	$610,609
Aug. "	96	122,809	29	18,838	139	92,783	203	77,103	500	218,445	967	529,978
Sept. "	142	170,973	205	108,797	378	267,339	718	275,371	698	359,655	2,141	1,182,135
Oct. "	241	269,229	31	17,443	289	173,754	260	95,527	356	181,285	1,177	737,238
Nov. "	307	378,056	41	20,825	1,022	661,053	1,296	521,330	1,193	550,070	3,859	2,131,334
Dec. "	244	287,512	14	8,592	519	352,534	309	127,176	1,021	594,251	2,107	1,370,065
Jan. 1882	207	263,886	37	19,324	327	237,372	666	274,172	345	179,717	1,582	974,471
Feb. "	169	206,340	11	352	751	496,611	335	133,120	500	279,059	1,756	1,115,482
March, "	58	181,172	159	65,364	598	385,868	283	106,412	614	344,201	1,712	1,083,017
April, "	265	325,306	1	577	1,070	699,172	210	81,215	619	316,591	2,165	1,422,861
May, "	309	379,568	16	5,828	650	432,088	224	91,166	512	249,920	1,711	1,158,570
June, "	160	211,148	16	6,010	544	362,132	70	28,287	544	254,561	1,334	862,138
TOTALS,	2,232	2,840,369	770	385,533	6,586	4,348,226	4,637	1,833,590	7,457	3,770,180	21,682	13,177,898

Compiled by the Secretary of the Silk Association of America, 416 Broome Street, New York.

IMPORTS OF RAW SILK AT NEW YORK AND SAN FRANCISCO, SEPARATE,
FOR THE FISCAL YEAR ENDING JUNE 30TH, 1882.

Months.	To New York.		To San Francisco.		Months.	To New York.		To San Francisco.	
	Bales.	Value.	Bales.	Value.		Bales.	Value.	Bales.	Value.
July, 1881	1,158	$ 604,817	13	$ 5,792	Jan. 1882	1,568	$ 966,569	14	$ 7,992
Aug. "	956	525,043	11	4,935	Feb. "	1,742	1,106,948	14	8,534
Sept. "	2,132	1,177,104	9	5,031	Mar. "	1,712	1,083,017	....	....
Oct. "	1,177	737,238	....	....	April "	2,152	1,415,997	13	6,864
Nov. "	3,833	2,120,600	26	10,734	May "	1,699	1,152,394	12	6,176
Dec. "	2,105	1,368,713	2	1,359	June "	1,316	853,616	18	8,522

Totals: to New York, 21,550 Bales, $13,112,056; to San Francisco, 132 Bales, $65,842.

IMPORTS OF WASTE SILK & PIERCED COCOONS AT THE PORTS OF NEW YORK & SAN FRANCISCO,
IN THE FISCAL YEARS ENDING JUNE 30TH.

Months.	1881–1882.		1880–1881.		1879–1880.		1878–1879.		1877–1878.		1876–1877.	
	Bales.	Value.	Bales.	Value.	Bales.	Value.	Bales.	Value.	Bales.	Value.	Bales.	Value.
July,	69	$ 53,086	....	....	2	$ 246	26	$ 7,569	89	$ 36,456	69	$ 19,101
August,	240	87,205	28	$ 12,590	164	50,872	6	9,000	3	1,200	....	....
September,	13	8,266	20	6,155	441	209,533	....	....	95	22,198	18	4,980
October,	50	24,498	17	8,828	1,584	412,286	1	300	467	105,277	2	1,000
November,	88	39,471	42	14,212	1,055	300,441	34	10,469	485	103,034	....	....
December,	187	63,721	19	8,264	338	78,573	30	20,148	550	121,242	50	15,783
January,	469	161,819	78	30,763	177	73,924	....	....	102	19,095	106	11,487
February,	142	16,871	12	4,872	70	12,604	35	2,702	56	29,101	334	164,171
March,	391	145,178	327	138,492	50	16,210	67	30,007	196	40,048	189	71,334
April,	7	3,537	647	178,949	10	6,939	29	14,604	189	57,891	33	11,391
May,	318	121,591	266	120,258	32	16,781	100	48,380	68	20,904	94	39,687
June,	3	1,935	33	19,515	27	28,097	14	6,187	6	2,112	85	16,345
Totals	1,977	727,268	1,489	542,898	3,950	1,206,506	342	141,292	2,306	558,558	980	355,279

Compiled by the Secretary of the Silk Association of America, 446 Broome Street, New York.

IMPORTS OF SILK MANUFACTURES AT THE PORT OF NEW YORK,
IN THE CALENDAR YEARS.

ARTICLES.	1881.	1880.	1879.	1878.	1877.	1876.	1875.	1874.	1873.	1872.
Silk Piece-Goods,	$16,959,043	$17,665,038	$15,104,026	$11,834,931	$11,978,135	$12,707,192	$12,639,397	$10,581,299	$9,764,650	$11,080,001
Satins,	243,273	267,929	202,672	50,219	26,795	41,403	107,501	250,756	205,524	334,403
Crapes,	517,795	443,238	435,662	372,231	397,995	504,277	470,806	641,380	577,575	459,727
Pongees,	13,499	8,205	1,996	394	2,617	......	10,126	2,629	561	......
Plushes,	898,553	408,219	125,487	101,198	73,777	85,668	125,722	127,045	221,421	309,485
Velvets,	1,255,091	2,044,139	1,976,133	1,510,240	1,049,305	1,384,450	1,151,427	1,087,131	888,143	1,512,590
Ribbons,	2,614,918	3,563,848	2,180,260	1,829,838	1,689,413	1,837,537	2,984,271	3,180,647	4,740,040	8,307,009
Laces,	2,909,193	1,540,892	1,059,969	921,265	1,158,689	1,248,740	1,039,055	1,708,181	1,960,672	2,218,452
Embroideries,	......	......	......	......	2,020	......	699	1,224	2,644	985
Shawls,	8,268	20,677	11,179	5,519	5,611	5,831	71,981	151	5,345	9,236
Gloves,	184,499	228,338	126,284	112,941	41,189	29,812	46,622	23,571	40,396	17,337
Cravats,	63,233	93,339	115,441	101,049	55,777	50,271	411,689	186,730	115,663	173,742
Handkerchiefs,	72,541	64,077	54,688	48,761	49,932	46,294	117,368	38,754	25,862	23,357
Mantillas,	......	......	......	......	......	573	......	......	......	......
Vestings,	......	......	......	......	......	2,427	3,625	2,467	53,431	66,621
Hose,	126,825	118,838	89,997	48,955	34,128	55,618	46,790	26,958	42,323	34,836
Threads and Yarns,	189,215	239,072	194,103	50,632	81,764	16,557	11,367	37,898	31,611	51,030
Braids and Bindings,	1,190,260	1,646,868	1,343,760	935,933	1,143,737	964,883	1,200,555	1,038,320	1,033,906	1,044,644
Silk and Worsted,	120,579	199,854	156,293	136,065	136,194	165,714	421,791	476,561	599,967	707,176
Silk and Cotton,	4,267,394	4,751,946	2,652,228	1,981,899	1,992,033	2,034,823	2,312,654	3,876,952	4,064,077	6,253,392
Silk and Linen,	2,495	943	651	660	3,720	10,316	3,689	3,897	5,511	73,726
TOTAL,	31,636,377	33,305,460	25,830,829	20,042,730	19,922,741	21,192,386	23,168,118	23,292,551	24,379,322	32,677,749

Compiled by the Secretary of the Silk Association of America, 46 Broome Street, New York.

IMPORTS OF SILK MANUFACTURES ENTERED AT THE PORT OF NEW YORK, IN FISCAL YEARS ENDING JUNE 30TH.

ARTICLES.	1881–1882.	1880–1881.	1879–1880.	1878–1879.	1877–1878.	1876–1877.	1875–1876.
Silk Piece-Goods,	$19,429,666	$16,167,056	$16,696,145	$13,877,796	$11,281,968	$12,647,212	$12,848,799
Satins,	200,763	272,641	263,591	113,705	33,081	28,460	67,672
Crapes,	536,277	489,560	457,071	434,744	324,040	517,014	416,046
Pongees,	8,651	16,477	3,212	1,996	580	2,431	
Plushes,	1,121,990	495,496	212,176	130,657	57,963	80,731	80,277
Velvets,	1,402,663	1,575,715	2,207,296	1,713,879	1,221,545	1,398,787	1,202,503
Ribbons,	2,707,693	3,103,564	2,975,147	1,995,257	1,640,647	1,524,724	2,749,208
Laces,	4,073,891	1,883,236	1,295,017	944,530	1,064,437	1,033,228	1,236,715
Embroideries,					1,552	468	
Shawls,	7,790	17,466	13,908	9,978	1,057	5,650	7,056
Gloves,	170,151	204,703	223,265	106,483	104,970	30,591	34,634
Cravats,	60,341	69,914	117,996	121,555	63,881	51,066	134,876
Handkerchiefs,	75,671	53,727	65,135	47,248	41,926	67,278	98,876
Mantillas,							573
Vestings,						1,616	811
Hose,	179,254	110,277	106,596	60,646	45,686	51,381	54,400
Threads and Yarns,	128,790	175,627	303,215	59,563	85,924	35,456	15,441
Braids and Bindings,	1,191,140	1,323,437	1,707,114	1,002,042	1,129,209	992,549	996,639
Silk and Worsted,	123,932	174,390	135,434	158,995	125,121	141,062	179,893
Silk and Cotton,	5,011,843	4,366,921	3,813,793	2,244,018	1,852,105	2,092,326	2,075,231
Silk and Linen,	2,253	1,644	398	811	2,969	7,555	7,206
Totals,	36,432,706	30,501,851	30,596,509	23,023,903	19,078,661	20,709,585	22,206,856

Compiled by the Secretary of the Silk Association of America, 446 Broome Street, New York.

IMPORTS OF SILK MANUFACTURES ENTERED AT THE PORT OF NEW YORK, BY MONTHS.
IN THE FISCAL YEAR ENDING JUNE 30TH, 1882.

Months	Silk Pc. G'ds.	Satins	Crapes	Pongees	Plushes	Velvets	Ribbons	Laces	Shawls
July, 1881	$1,389,885	$16,333	$61,028	......	$104,928	$205,495	$113,445	$303,300	$ 233
Aug. "	2,120,962	26,254	48,802	$ 754	139,305	260,722	369,713	430,810	2,159
Sept. "	1,950,410	21,063	43,533	......	131,524	187,066	241,530	275,613	......
Oct. "	1,588,009	14,201	35,939	......	119,159	121,976	196,608	246,255	696
Nov. "	1,295,959	12,986	20,425	......	147,248	85,033	165,347	251,142	......
Dec. "	940,198	12,098	32,052	1,261	36,912	52,490	150,539	247,462	1,051
Jan. 1882	1,627,707	23,172	75,644	2,581	20,546	34,460	263,372	356,002	14
Feb. "	1,906,651	7,957	51,863	......	26,472	41,730	345,805	325,898	1,711
Mar. "	2,524,600	22,934	50,525	......	64,578	67,571	317,017	372,626	527
April, "	1,740,102	13,447	56,340	2,032	72,529	44,861	219,172	357,489	439
May, "	1,470,666	19,332	20,478	......	115,408	132,326	188,600	610,927	314
June, "	874,457	10,386	39,642	2,019	143,381	168,933	127,545	296,367	666
Totals,	19,429,606	200,763	536,277	8,651	1,121,990	1,402,663	2,707,693	4,073,891	7,799

Months	Gloves	Cravats	Handkchfs.	Hose	Thrd. & Yrn.	Braid & Bdgs.	Silk & Wstd.	Silk & Cotton	Silk & Linen	Totals
July, 1881	$ 1,086	$11,953	$13,096	$ 6,785	$12,630	$105,327	$ 3,823	$341,741	......	$2,691,088
Aug. "	7,155	9,386	16,590	26,967	33,861	180,865	15,324	569,481	$157	4,259,267
Sept. "	5,748	4,850	8,738	15,768	15,380	116,272	15,183	407,055	575	3,441,208
Oct. "	6,763	2,135	5,550	14,073	16,185	84,564	17,069	381,785	228	2,861,195
Nov. "	1,705	2,340	8,585	5,565	11,892	80,491	7,592	364,426	136	2,460,872
Dec. "	4,110	2,341	2,575	6,695	13,915	71,319	6,416	308,770	......	2,866,204
Jan. 1882	35,649	9,452	5,350	21,398	10,021	100,228	13,289	464,080	......	3,062,769
Feb. "	28,185	4,062	3,154	21,493	7,961	127,845	11,255	493,458	354	3,408,854
Mar. "	25,918	2,693	1,468	22,236	328	99,266	9,670	671,248	803	4,253,948
April, "	22,484	483	3,114	19,506	1,368	73,765	4,786	305,517	......	2,935,210
May, "	22,250	4,686	2,885	12,254	1,773	90,076	6,730	419,250	......	3,117,955
June, "	9,098	5,960	4,566	6,424	3,476	61,182	2,802	287,032	......	2,043,936
Totals,	170,151	60,341	75,671	179,254	128,790	1,191,140	123,939	5,011,843	2,253	36,432,706

Compiled by the Secretary of the Silk Association of America, 446 Broome Street, New York.

WOOL AND WOOLEN MANUFACTURES, DUTIES IN DETAIL.

ARTICLES.	VALUES.	DUTIES.	Duty reduced to ad val. Per Cent.
Clothing Wools, Class No. 1, Raw or Unmanufactured	$4,751,453.79	2,599,685.83	54.71
Combing Wools, " 2, " "	1,271,332.39	585,499.93	46.05
Carpet Wools, " 3, " "	6,038,040.72	1,675,629.64	27.75
Carpets and Carpeting	1,400,062.59	817,068.50	58.36
Dress Goods—women's and children's	15,961,065.74	10,734,061.81	67.25
Balmorals	25,044.00	19,104.05	76.28
Blankets	1,954.44	1,492.10	76.34
Flannels	17,628.66	16,240.79	92.12
Hosiery	827,557.56	461,613.31	55.78
Manufactures of Wool not otherwise specified	1,553,036.42	1,098,363.27	70.72
Shirts, Drawers and other Knit Goods	178,685.50	121,442.91	67.96
Manufactures of Wool and Worsted—Bunting	28.40	21.94	77.25
" " " " —Cloths	9,376,037.72	6,810,073.89	72.63
Clothing—Articles of Wear	174,135.74	97,940.38	56.24
" —Ready-made	834,054.17	489,051.31	58.64
Belts and Felts for Machines	123,065.00	72,120.65	58.59
Hats	994.63	599.34	60.26
Rags, Waste, Shoddy, Mungo and Flocks	160,498.00	65,174.01	40.61
Shawls—Woolen and Worsted	1,176,198.00	683,917.67	58.15
Webbings, Fishing Bindings, Braid, Fringes &c.	327,321.00	223,443.64	68.26
Yarns	540,096.83	424,900.85	78.67
Other Manufactures, wholly or in part of wool	425,857.71	288,178.96	67.67
TOTAL	45,164,149.01	27,285,624.78	60.41

SUGAR, MOLASSES &c., DUTIES IN DETAIL.

ARTICLES.	VALUES.	DUTIES.	Duty reduced to ad val. Per Cent.
Sugar	82,721,087.27	45,933,045.09	55.53
Molasses	6,366,177.15	1,659,064.14	26.06
Sirup, Concentrated Molasses and Melada	715,358.00	385,028.40	53.82
Sugar Candy and Confectionery	9,163.06	6,895.21	75.25
TOTAL	89,811,785.48	47,984,032.84	53.43

SILK MANUFACTURES, DUTIES IN DETAIL.

ARTICLES.	VALUES.	DUTY.	Duty Pr. Ct.
Braids, Laces, Fringes and Galloons	$2,509,253.00	$1,505,551.80	60.00
Buttons and Ornaments	31,114.00	18,501.60	59.46
Dress and Piece-goods	18,591,526.67	11,154,916.01	60.00
Floss	5,543.00	1,940.05	35.00
Hats, Caps and Bonnets	45,659.00	27,395.40	60.00
Hosiery	454,512.00	272,707.20	60.00
Pongees and Vestings	2,222.00	1,333.20	60.00
Ready-made Clothing	440,715.22	264,429.13	60.00
Ribbons	2,390,799.00	1,434,479.40	60.00
" edge of cotton	645,829.00	322,914.50	50.00
Sewing-silk in the gum or purified	103,463.00	41,385.20	40.00
Shawls	1,520.00	912.00	60.00
Silk and India-rubber, Manufactures of, Silk component of chief value	22,288.00	13,372.80	60.00
" " " 25 per cent of other material	838.00	419.00	50.00
Silk in the gum, not more advanced than tram or organzine	6,734.00	2,356.90	35.00
Silk manufactures not otherwise specified, Silk of chief value	2,679,587.33	1,607,752.39	60.00
" " " " 25 per cent of other textiles	2,683,072.26	1,341,536.13	50.00
Spun Silk, for filling, in skeins or cops	60,839.00	21,290.50	35.00
Twist	77,800.00	31,120.00	40.00
Velvets	1,623,921.00	974,352.60	60.00
TOTALS	32,377,226.48	19,038,665.81	58.80

MANUFACTURES OF COTTON, DUTIES IN DETAIL.

ARTICLES.	VALUES.	DUTY.	Duty Pr ct.
Plain Bleached: not over 20 cents per square yard	$1,122,984.00	$499,733.04	44.50
" " over " " " "	3.30	1.15	34.85
Not Bleached: not over 16 cents " "	19,609.00	8,551.85	43.60
Printed or Colored: not over 25 cents per square yard, or 100 threads to inch	7,618.99	3,324.60	43.64
" " " " " " 200 " "	453,843.00	263,460.71	58.05
" " " over " " 200 " "	46,858.00	27,192.54	58.03
" " " " " " " "	613.95	214.88	35.00
Hosiery	8,185,959.10	2,865,085.69	35.00
Jeans, Denims, Drillings, Tickings, Ginghams, Cottonades, Bleached: not over 20 cts. pr. sq. yd., or 200 thrds. to inch	81,022.00	36,705.72	45.30
" " " " over " " " "	13,711.00	6,215.94	45.33
" " " Not Bleached " " "	2,303.80	814.38	35.35
" " " " " over " " " "	323.00	106.40	32.94
" " " Printed, Painted or Colored, not over 100 thrds. to inch	126,727.39	56,220.34	44.76
" " " " " " " " 200 " "	1,454,965.00	760,230.17	52.25
" " " " " over " " 200 " "	79,036.00	46,110.14	58.34
Laces, Cords, Braids, Gimps, Galloons, Insertings	5,124,102.76	1,793,435.96	35.00
Ready-made Clothing	465,870.13	163,054.55	35.00
Shirts or Drawers woven or made on frames	21,518.78	7,531.57	35.00
Thread on spools, not exceeding 100 yards	43,259.50	32,417.76	74.94
" " " exceeding 100 yards	48,943.50	38,435.30	78.54
Thread, Yarn, Warps, not on spools, and not over 40 cents per lb	108,235.00	52,361.26	48.38
" " " " " 60 " "	267,455.00	156,004.24	58.33
" " " " " 80 " "	537,719.00	339,110.16	61.39
" " " " over 80 cents per lb	1,173,613.00	633,459.94	53.98
Other Cotton Yarn or Warp, on spools	104,832.00	36,691.20	35.00
Velvets, Velveteens, Velvet Ribbons, Bindings and Vestings	1,154,573.00	404,100.55	35.00
Waste and Flocks	2,693.00	538.60	20.00
Manufactures of Cotton not otherwise provided for	7,435,724.49	2,602,503.57	35.00
TOTAL	28,084,116.69	10,825,115.21	38.55

DUTY-PAYING IMPORTS OF THE UNITED STATES.
HOME CONSUMPTION.—FOR THE YEAR ENDING JUNE 30TH, 1881.

ARTICLES.	VALUE.	DUTY.	TARIFF.	Duty reduced to Ad Valorem. Per Cent.	Proportion of Total Duties. Per Cent.
Sugar, Molasses and Confectionery,	$89,811,785.48	$47,984,032.84	mixed.	53.43	24.79
Wool, and manufactures of,	45,164,149.01	27,285,624.78	"	60.42	14.09
Iron and Steel, and manufactures of,	51,454,573.60	21,462,534.34	"	41.71	11.09
Silk, manufactures of,	32,377,226.48	19,038,665.81	ad. val.	58.80	9.84
Cotton, manufactures of,	28,084,116.69	10,825,115.21	mixed.	38.55	5.59
Flax, manufactures of,	21,020,570.62	6,984,374.90	ad. val.	33.23	3.61
Spirits and Wines,	8,762,762.74	6,471,641.54	mixed.	73.85	3.34
Tobacco, and manufactures of,	6,474,938.67	4,655,591.67	"	71.90	2.40
Chemicals, Drugs, Dyes and Medicines,	14,888,493.15	4,635,261.10	"	31.13	2.40
Tin, manufactures of,	14,714,146.53	4,194,690.33	"	28.51	2.17
Fruits, including nuts,	12,511,806.39	3,341,848.66	"	26.71	1.73
Leather, and manufactures of,	10,522,601.24	3,337,034.44	ad. val.	31.71	1.72
Glass, and manufactures of,	5,862,269.60	3,296,541.42	mixed.	56.23	1.70
Fancy articles, perfumery &c.,	7,084,301.69	2,934,850.75	ad. val.	41.43	1.52
Breadstuffs &c.,	9,208,956.23	2,762,128.48	mixed.	29.99	1.43
Earthenware and China,	6,383,874.27	2,727,476.43	ad. val.	42.73	1.40
Hemp, Jute &c., and manufactures of,	10,568,126.16	2,261,997.78	mixed.	21.40	1.17
Wood, and manufactures of,	7,496,815.79	1,536,024.59	"	20.49	.79
Embroideries,	3,133,590.00	1,096,756.50	ad. val.	35.00	.57
Spices,	2,203,078.49	1,095,139.10	specific.	49.71	.57
Salt,	1,908,797.19	920,056.90	"	48.20	.48
Buttons and Button materials,	3,160,419.85	912,134.96	ad. val.	28.86	.47
Furs, and manufactures of,	4,270,161.33	911,021.87	"	21.34	.47

Diamonds, cameos, mosaics &c.,	8,330,071.45	835,052.19	ad. val.	10.02	.43
Animals, living,	3,917,823.93	783,564.69	"	20.00	.40
Braids, plaits, flats, laces, trimmings &c.,	2,340,384.00	702,115.20	"	30.00	.36
Clocks and Watches,	2,447,399.34	647,657.14	"	26.46	.33
Books, engravings, prints &c.,	2,560,588.99	635,229.87	"	24.81	.33
Paper, and manufactures of,	1,806,891.06	619,832.86	"	34.30	.32
Coal,	2,073,954.78	516,006.95	specific.	24.88	.27
Fish,	1,355,724.88	469,352.65	"	34.62	.24
Oils, mineral, animal and vegetable,	1,051,683.43	417,698.36	mixed.	39.72	.22
Musical instruments &c.,	1,390,391.02	417,342.25	ad. val.	30.02	.22
Hats, bonnets and hoods,	982,943.55	393,177.41	"	40.00	.20
Metals, and manufactures of,	1,162,913.05	343,191.25	"	29.52	.18
Paints and colors,	985,604.69	342,782.39	mixed.	34.78	.18
Beer, ale and porter,	848,958.80	341,185.62	specific.	40.19	.18
Marble, and manufactures of,	553,900.32	340,075.15	mixed.	61.40	.17
Seeds,	1,612,207.41	277,977.45	"	17.24	.14
Provisions, not otherwise specified,	1,127,874.98	244,089.19	"	21.64	.13
Paintings &c., not by American artists,	2,210,944.47	223,802.35	ad. val.	10.12	.12
Copper, and manufactures of,	564,923.54	210,307.66	mixed.	37.23	.11
Corsets and corset-cloths,	535,819.00	187,571.30	"	35.01	.10
Hair, and manufactures of,	734,055.55	173,964.89	ad. val.	23.70	.09
Mats and matting,	519,128.29	153,902.58	"	29.65	.08
Vegetables, not otherwise specified,	746,510.07	151,470.08	mixed.	20.29	.08
Brass, and manufactures of,	494,249.01	140,438.51	ad. val.	28.41	.07
Soap,	252,751.35	117,968.00	mixed.	46.67	.06
Zinc, and manufactures of,	262,218.48	106,914.20	"	40.77	.05
All other dutiable articles,	10,124,111.31	3,097,796.58		30.59	1.60
TOTALS,	448,061,587.95	193,561,011.17		43.20	100.00

Clercy, Joseph A. Silk Throwster .... Mansfield
Gardner & Pierce. Machine Twist and Sewing Silk.
Mills at .... Conantville and Willimantic
Globe Silk Works. Marvin & Pardee. Machine Twist, Sewing, Floss and Embroidery Silks, Organzine and Tram. Factory and salesroom, cor. State and Wall Sts .... New Haven
Hammond & Knowlton. Sewing Silk, Machine and Button-hole Twist. Salesroom, 524 Broadway, New York. Mills .... Putnam
Hanks, P. G. & J. S. Machine Twist .... Gurleyville
Hartford Silk Manufacturing Co. T. F. Plunkett, President; E. A. Freeman, Secretary and Treasurer. Tapestry and Piece Goods. Root & Childs, 45 Leonard St., New York, Selling Agents. Mill ...... Tariffville
Heminway, M. & Son's Silk Co. M. Heminway, President; H. Heminway, Treasurer. Sewing Silk and Machine Twist, Embroidery, Saddlers', Knitting and Filling Silks. Salesrooms, 78 Reade and 99 Church Sts., New York; 14 North 5th St., Phila. Mills .... Watertown
Holland Manufacturing Co. Ira Dimock, Manager; S. L. Burlingham, Attorney. Sewing Silk and Machine Twist. Salesrooms, H. Eldridge, Agent, 435 Broadway, New York; 19 High St., Boston; 633 Market St., Philadelphia. Mills .... Willimantic
Jackson, F. L. Silk Dyer ....Mansfield Centre
Leigh & White. Tram and Knitting Silk .... New Haven
Lauderbach & Daggett. Sewing Silk and Machine Twist. Salesroom, 472 Broadway, New York. Mill. New Haven
Leonard Silk Co. Sewing Silk and Machine Twist. J. H. Simonds, President and Treasurer, Warehouse Point, Conn. Salesrooms, 140 Church St., New York; 41 High St., Boston; 414 Arch St., Philadelphia; 27 German St., Baltimore. Mills ...... Warehouse Point
Macfarlane, James S. Sewing Silk, Machine and Button-hole Twists. Salesroom, 24 Walker St., New York. Mills .... Mansfield Centre
Merrick and Conant Manufacturing Co. Sewing Silk, Machine Twist and Spool Cotton; also Silk Throwsters .... Easthampton
Morgan & Bottum. Machine Twist .... .South Coventry
New England Silk Co. Capital, $50,000 .... Winchester

New London Silk Weaving Co. A. L. Washburn,
    Henry P. Gray and John Gray, Corporators........ New London
Osborn, W. H.   Silk Braid.... ... . Willimantic
Pardee, C. H., & J. H. Booth. Coach Laces and Car-
    riage Trimmings, 9 Wooster St.................... New Haven
Patterson, Erbacher & Co.   Dress Silks, Brocades,
    Satins. Salesroom, 75 Greene St., New York......
    Factory.. Bridgeport
Robinson, L. P. Sewing Silk.....................South Coventry
Smith, E. B. Machine Twist. Belding Bros. & Co.,
    Selling Agents, 456 Broadway, New York. Mill.... Gurleyville
Tunxis Silk Co. Thomas F. Plunkett, President; John
    L. Gray, Secretary; A. L. Hedden, Treasurer; Wm.
    O. Atwood, General Manager...................... Tariffville
Turner, P. W. & Son. Ribbons, Handkerchiefs, Gum
    Silk and Machine Twist. Salesroom, 27 Greene St.,
    New York. Mills................................ Turnerville
Washburn, Alanson. Fringe Silk.................South Coventry
Williams, William E. Sewing Silk and Machine Twist. Gurleyville
Willimantic Silk Co. John M. Hall, President; Wm.
    H. Osborn, Treasurer. Hat Bands and Bindings... Willimantic
Winsted Silk Co. Eugene Potter, Manager. Machine
    and Button-hole Twist, and Sewing, Embroidery
    and Floss Silks. Agencies in Boston and Chicago..West Winsted

ILLINOIS.

CHICAGO.

Aub, Hackenburg & Co. (See *Philadelphia, Pa.*) Sales-
    room,.....................................152 Fifth Av.
Baum & Ernst. Fringes, Cords, Tassels, Gimps. Fac-
    tory and salesroom ....150-154 Fifth Av.
Belding Bros. & Co. (See *Rockville, Conn.*) Sales-
    rooms...147-149 Fifth Av.
Betts, Clark & Co. Sewing Silks.................... Chicago.
Cutter, John D. & Co. (See *Newark, N. J.*) Sales-
    room..127 Fifth Av.
Eureka Silk Manufacturing Co. (See *Canton, Mass.*)
    Salesroom.....................................115 Fifth Av.
Fiedler, A. B. Dress Trimmings, Fringes, Gimps, Or-
    naments, Cord Tassels and Buttons. Factory, 449-
    451 N. Wells St. Salesroom.................48 E. Madison St.

Foster, G. F., Son & Co.   Cords, Fringes, Tassels,
  Society and Military Trimmings. Office......23 Washington St.
Gossage, Charles & Co.   Dress Trimmings.   Agency,
  cor. Church and Worth Sts., New York.   Factory
  and salesroom...................................... 108 State St.
Heuer & Brockschmidt.   Dealers in Upholstery Trimmings... 16 Fifth Av.
Jacobs, W. W. & Co.   Fringes, Tassels, Cords, Upholstery and Drapery Trimmings..............185-187 Wabash Av.
Kursheedt Manufacturing Co. (See *New York*.) Salesrooms...87-89 Wabash Av.
Lipper, M. W. & Co. (See *Philadelphia, Pa.*) Salesroom ....144 Wabash Av.
Nonotuck Silk Co. (See *Florence, Mass.*) Salesroom..207-209 Fifth Av.
Peters, M.   Upholstery Trimmings, Cords, Tassels and
  Fringes.................................61 Washington St.
Skinner, Wm. (See *Holyoke, Mass.*)   Salesroom.....144 Fifth Av.
Stevenson, J. H. & Co.   Fringes and Tassels........   Chicago.

KANSAS.

Boissière, E. V.   Ribbons and Dress Trimmings ; also
  Silk Culture....................Silkville, Williamsburgh P. O.

MAINE.

Downs & Adams Silk Manufacturing Co. (See *Athol,
  Mass.*) Office...   Portland
Haskell Silk Co.   James Haskell, President ; Frank
  Haskell, Treasurer.   Sewing Silk, Machine Twist,
  Organzine, Tram, Fringe Silk and Gros-grain Dress
  Goods. E. A. Kingman, Selling Agent, 36 Lispenard St., New York. Mills......................   Saccarappa

MARYLAND.

BALTIMORE.

Aub, Hackenburg & Co. (See *Philadelphia, Pa.*) Salesroom.. 19 Light St.
Brainerd & Armstrong Co. (See *New London, Conn.*)
  Salesroom................................35 Sharpe St.

Carpenter, John.   Fringes and Undertakers' Trimmings..88 South Eutaw St.
Leonard Silk Co. (See *Warehouse Point, Conn.*) Salesroom...27 German St.
Munder, Theophilus.   Upholstery Trimmings......81 Lexington St.
Sisco Bros.   Trimmings, Flags and Regalia.......50 N. Charles St.
Stern, S. L. & Co.   Dress and Upholstery Trimmings, Piece Goods and Neckwear. Office, 101 German St. Factory..................................43 German St.
Tallerman, Gustav.   Fringes and Dress Trimmings.
                                       150 Lexington St., cor. Howard.
Wells, Mrs. F. M.   Undertakers' Trimmings......321 Lombard St

MASSACHUSETTS.

BOSTON.

Abercrombie, Geo. N.   Fringes, Cords, Tassels, Buttons, etc. Office and Factory..................129 Tremont St.
Adams, C. E.   Dealer in Sewing Silk...............   Boston.
Barr, Rider & Co.   Dealers in Sewing Silks........21 Summer St.
Belding Bros. & Co. (See *Rockville, Conn.*) Salesroom..105 Summer St.
Benedict, W. H. (See *New Brunswick, N. J.*) Salesroom of Selling Agents..........................18 Summer St.
Boston Elastic Fabric Co. (See *Chelsea, Mass.*) Salesroom...175 Devonshire St.
Brown, L. D., & Son. (See *Middletown, Conn.*) Salesroom..27 Lincoln St.
Burr, Brown & Co. (See *Hingham, Mass.*) Salesrooms.......................163 Devonshire and 24 Arch Sts.
Cutter, John D. & Co. (See *Newark, N. J.*) Salesroom, 6 Bedford St.
Downs & Adams. (See *Athol, Mass.*) Salesroom...5 Chauncey St.
Eureka Silk Manufacturing Co. (See *Canton, Mass.*)
   Seavey, Foster & Bowman, Agents.   Salesroom...40 Summer St.
Farwell, Isaac, Jr. & Co. (See *Watertown, Mass.*)
   Salesroom.......................................   92 Arch St.
Fiedler, Moeldner & Co.   Dress and Cloak Trimmings.   Factory, Roxbury. Salesroom..........60 Summer St.
French, A. W.   Dealer in Gum Silks...............19 Summer St.
Glendale Elastic Fabric Co. (See *Easthampton, Mass.*)
   Salesroom of Selling Agents ....   10 Milk St.
Holland Manufacturing Co. (See *Willimantic, Conn.*)
   Salesroom ....   19 High St.

SILK GOODS DIRECTORY.—MASSACHUSETTS. 113

Hubbard, **Dudley.** Fringes, Cords, Tassels and Buttons... 22 Winter St.
Kelsea, Joseph **N.** (See *Antrim, N. H.*) Salesroom of Selling Agent.............................179 Washington St.
Knight, Geo. **W.** (See *Newtown, Mass.*) Salesroom..28 Lincoln St.
Leonard **Silk Co.** (See *Warehouse Point, Conn.*) Salesroom... 41 High St.
Linneman, C. A. Silks, Fringes and Trimmings....28 Chauncy St.
Messinger, V. J. & Co. Dealers in Sewing Silk and Machine Twist.. 23 Dock Sq.
Newry, Joshua E. **Skein Silk** Dyer......812 Albany St., Roxbury.
Nonotuck Silk Co. (See *Florence, Mass.*) Salesroom.18 Summer St.
Polhaus, Ernest. Silk Dyer.................... .. Jamaica Plains.
Schoenfuss, **F.** & Co. **Fringes,** Buttons and Cords.383 Washington St.
Seavey, **Foster & Bowman.** (See *Eureka Manufacturing Co., Canton, Mass.*)............................40 Summer St.
Streeter & Mayhew. (See *Shelburne Falls, Mass.*) Salesroom of Selling Agent..................... 37 High St.
Whitney, H. L. Dealer in Sewing Silk.............. Boston.
Wilkins, **Thomas & Co.** Sewing Silk **Dealers, Greene St.,** nr Bowdoin
Ziegler, **Alfred.** Suspender Web, Upholstery Trimmings, **Fringes, Gimps** and **Silk** Ties. Factory, Decatur Av., cor. of Pynchon St. Salesroom......**5 Chauncy St.**
Ziegler, Conrad. Silk **Dyer**............,......54 George St., Roxbury

MASSSACHUSETTS—(Continued.)

Belding Bros. & Co. (See *Rockville, Conn.*) **Mill** ... Northampton
Boston Elastic Fabric Co. **Suspenders,** Garter **Webs,**
Frills. Salesrooms, 175 Devonshire St., **Boston,** and 332 Broadway, New York. **Factory** .... Chelsea
Bottum, **C. L. Silk** Dyer..................... ... Northampton
Bottum & Trescott. Machine Twist and Sewing Silk.
Salesroom, 55 Walker St., New **York.** Mill........ Springfield
Burr, **Brown & Co.** Fringes, **Gimps,** Cords, Tassels, and Carriage, **Military** and **Upholstery** Trimmings. Salesrooms, 163 **Devonshire** and **24 Arch Sts.,** Boston. Factory.. Hingham
Downs & Adams Silk Manufacturing Co. Henry **W. Downs,** President ; **Thomas** H. Goodspeed, Athol, Mass., **Treasurer** and Assistant **Secretary ; J. A.**

Hayden, Secretary; Daniel E. Adams, 48 Walker St., New York, General Sales Agent. Sewing Silk and Machine Twist. Offices, 5 Chauncy St., Boston, Portland, Me., and New York. Factory.......... Athol

Eureka Silk Manufacturing Co. J. W. C. Seavey, President; F. A. Foster, Secretary; John A. Bowman, Treasurer. Sewing Silk, Machine Twist and Embroidery Silks. Salesrooms, 7 Mercer St., New York; 40 Summer St., Boston; 115 Fifth Av., Chicago; 707 Washington Av., St. Louis. Mills............... Canton

Farwell, Isaac, Jr., & Co. Sewing Silk and Machine Twist. Salesroom, 92 Arch St., Boston. Mill..... Watertown

Glendale Elastic Fabric Co. Joseph W. Green, Jr., Treasurer. Elastic Shoe Gorings, Cords, Braids and Garter Webs. Stoddard, Lovering & Co., 10 Milk St., Boston, and 8 Thomas St., New York, Selling Agents. Factory............................... Easthampton

Glenwood Mills. O. G. Webster and A. S. King. Dress Goods, Organzine and Tram, and Machine Silks. C. G. Landon & Co., 419-421 Broome St., New York, Selling Agents. Mills................. Easthampton

Gold Medal Braid Co. H. A. Daggett, President. Silk Fishing Lines. Factory.....................Attleborough Falls

King, Albert. Silk Dyer........................... Florence

Knight, Geo. W. Naumkeag Spool Silk. Office, 38 Lincoln St., Boston. Factory..................... Newtown

Lathrop Bros. Sewing Silk, Machine Twist and Fringe Silk. Mills and Salesroom. .... Northampton

Mansfield, G. H. & Co. Braided Fishing Lines...... Canton

Nonotuck Silk Co. Ira Dimock, President; A. T. Lilly, Treasurer. Machine Twist, Sewing and Knitting Silks. Mills at Florence and Leeds, Mass. Salesrooms, 19 Mercer St., New York; 18 Summer St., Boston; 207-209 Fifth Av., Chicago; 317 North Fifth St., St. Louis; 88 West Third St., Cincinnati, and at Gloversville, N. Y. Principal mills......... Florence

Skinner, William & Son. Unquomonk Silk Mills. Sewing Silk, Machine Twist, Sleeve Linings, Serges, Silk and Mohair Braids and Bindings. Salesrooms, 508 Broadway, New York, and 144 Fifth Av., Chicago, Ill. Mills.. Holyoke

Smith & Rice. Sewings, Machine Twist and Braid. Agencies in Boston and New York. Mill.......... Pittsfield

Streeter & Mayhew. Machine Twist, Sewing Silk Fringe, Tram and Organzine. Agencies, H. H. Sanderson, 7 Mercer St., N. Y., and D. P. Bedell, 37 High St., Boston. Mills.....................Shelburne Falls

Warner, Luther J. Sewing Silk, Machine Twist and Embroidery Silk. Mills and Salesroom........... Northampton

Worcester Silk Co. E. M. Kennedy, Proprietor. Plain and Fancy Schappe Gros grain Ribbons. George R. Kennedy, Agent, Worcester, Mass. Mill.......... Worcester

MISSOURI.

Belding Bros. & Co. (See *Rockville, Conn.*) Salesroom, 603 Washington Av................................ St. Louis

Eureka Silk Manufacturing Co. (See *Canton, Mass.*) Salesroom, 707 Washington Av.................... St. Louis

Nonotuck Silk Co. (See *Florence, Mass.*) Salesrooms, 317 N. Fifth St.. St. Louis

Schacht & Bro. Dress Trimmings. 326 Market St.. St. Louis

NEW HAMPSHIRE.

Kelsea, Joseph N. Sewing Silk and Machine Twist. Agent, W. J. Baker, 179 Washington St., Boston. Mills and Salesroom............................. Antrim

NEW JERSEY.

PATERSON.

Adams, Robert & Co. Ribbons. Office, 10 Greene St., New York. Factory, Hamilton Mill.......... Mill St.

Adams, R. & H. Ribbons, Fancy Silks, Handkerchiefs, Mosquito Nets, Crinolines and Wiggins. Salesrooms, 83 and 85 Greene St., New York. Harmony Mills. Van Houten St.

Alcock, Frederick W. Dress Goods, Handkerchiefs, Grenadines, Tie Silks. Whitney & Matthews, 85 Leonard St., New York, Selling Agents. Factory, Dale Mill............................... .... Railroad Av.

American Braid Co. Benj. Curley & Co. Silk Watch Chains, etc............. .... Paterson

American Silk Finishing Co. Silk Finishers. Works.. Empire Mill

Anderson, John & Sons.   Handkerchiefs, Figured
 Dress Goods, Ties and Scarfs.   Jas. Talcott, Agent,
 108 and 110 Franklin St., New York. Totowa Mills. 48 Redwood St.
Armitt, T.   Hand-made Sewing Silk, Fish-lines and
 Glove Cord.   Factory.... ....Little Beaver Mill
Ashley & Bailey.   Tie Silks, Dress Goods and Handkerchiefs.   A. Person, Harriman & Co., 457-459
 Broome St., New York, Selling Agents.   Mills at
 Fort Plain, N. Y., and.... .... River St.
Auer, C. B.   Satins and Brocades.   Murray Mill, Mill
 St., and the Meyenberg Mill..................... Ward St.
Auerbach & Co.   Sewing Silk and Twist.   Salesroom,
 526 Broadway. New York.   Mill................. Paterson
Baare, Frederick.   Soft Silk Winding......166-168 Van Houten St.
Ball, William.   Handkerchiefs................. .... 93 River St.
Barnes & Peel.   Silk and Mohair Braids, Cords, Organzine and Tram.   Granite Mill.... .... Grand St.
Berry, William.   Dress Goods, Handkerchiefs. O'Blenis Hall, Arch St.
Booth, J. H. & Co.   Tram, Organzine, Floss and Sewings.   Office with Wm. Ryle, 54 Howard St., New
 York.   Mills................. ....cor. Market and Spruce Sts.
Bowles, Robert............. ....175 Marshall St.
Broomhall, Geo. L.   Dress Goods, Handkerchiefs and
 Millinery Silks.   Whitney & Matthews, 85 Leonard
 St., New York, Selling Agents.   Mill.... .... Warren St.
Bruchet, Louis.   Handkerchiefs.................... 93 River St.
Chapin, J. L.   Dress Goods and Handkerchiefs. Office,
 96 Reade St., New York.   A. D. Juilliard & Co., 66
 Worth St., New York, Selling Agents.   Factory..... Paterson
Colle, J.   Chenille............................ ...300 Main St.
Crescent Manufacturing Co.   Tram and Organzine,
 and Commission Throwsters.   Peter Ryle, Manager.
 Crescent Mill............................Rip Van Winkle Av.
Crew, Sons & Co.   Dyers and Silk Finishers.   104-106 Railroad Av.
Crouchley, C.   Handkerchiefs and Dress Goods.   Dale
 Mill............   .... Railroad Av.
Dale, Frederick S.   Silk and Mohair Braids and Bindings, and Commission Throwster.   Dale & Kimball,
 Agents, 419-421 Broadway, New York.   Dale Mill. Railroad Av.
Day, John.   Handkerchiefs .... 93 River St.
Day, Joseph.   Ribbons........................66 Mechanic St.
Dexter, Lambert & Co.   Ribbons, Dress Silks, etc.
 Dexter Mill and Lambert Mill, Paterson, N. J.;

Bellemont Mill and Nelson Mill, Hawley, Pa. Salesrooms, 33-35 Greene St., New York. Principal Mill at Straight St.................................... Paterson
Doherty & Wadsworth. Dress Goods, Handkerchiefs, and Millinery Silks. Selling Agents, Megroz, Portier, Grose & Co., 85-87 Grand St., New York. Arkwright Mill........................Beach and Morton Sts.
Dorgeval, P. Silk Looms. Dale Mill............ Railroad Av.
Dover Silk Manufacturing Co. Dress and Millinery Silks and Handkerchiefs........................ 9 Fair St.
Dunlop, John. Union Silk Works. Organzine, Tram, Sewing Silk, Machine Twist, Saddlers' and Embroidery Silks. Salesroom, 25 Mercer St., New York. Mill.........................Morton and Straight Sts.
Dunkerly & Co.............................. Paterson
Fletcher, John & Son. Silk Plush...............106 Straight St.
Fletcher, Joseph. Commission Throwster and Plush Manufacturer............................... 119 Tyler St.
Franke, Louis. Organzine, Tram, Twist, Fringe Silk and Braids, especially prepared for Trimming Manufacturers. Salesroom, 110 Grand St, New York. Factory........................cor. Bridge and River Sts.
Freeman, H. H. & Co. Broad Silks, Handkerchiefs and Grenadines. Mill............cor. Front and Rockland Sts.
Frost, George & Sons. Albion Mill. Thrown Silk; also Soft Silk Winding.....................36-42 Madison St.
Gazzera, A. Throwster....................... Haledon
Gianetti, G. Dress Goods. Barnet Mills........... Railroad Av.
Greenwood Bros. Commission Throwsters. Mill..51 Mechanic St.
Greenwood, Sam'l. Commission Throwster. Dale Mill..Railroad Av.
Gregson & McCulloch. Spun Silk. Philip Wamsley & Co., 353 Canal St., New York, Selling Agents. Factories at Sloatsburg, N. Y., and..........42 Van Houten St.
Greppo, Claude. Silk Dyer. Office, 27 Mercer St., New York. Works......................:......Riverside, Paterson
Grimshaw Bros. Grimshaw Mill. Handkerchiefs, Tie Silks, Scarfs, Dress and Millinery Silks. E. Oelbermann & Co., 57-63 Greene St., New York, Selling Agents. Mills,..........Dale Av., Slater and Prince Sts.
Grish, John. Broad Silks, Handkerchiefs, Millinery and Dress Trimmings. Grosvenor & Carpenter, 54-56 White St., and James Talcott, 108-110 Franklin St., New York, Selling Agents. Mill..........63 Railroad Av.

Hamil & Booth. Passaic Silk Works and Hamil Mill.
 Tram and Organzine, Fringe Silks, Millinery and
 Fancy Silks and Ribbons. Salesrooms, 96 and 98
 Grand St., New York. Office of Mills.......Ward St., Paterson
Hankin, Wm. H., Jr., & Co. Tie and Fancy Silks,
 Handkerchiefs, Grenadines...................... 22 Fair St.
Hawks, M. J. & Co. Prussian Bindings, Galloons, etc.,
 M. H. Chapin, Agent, 81 Greene St., New York.
 Hamilton Mill................................. Mill St.
Holmes, W. D. Dress Goods, Handkerchiefs, etc... 11½ Fair St.
Hopper, C. C. Dress Goods and Handkerchiefs.
 Watson Mill................................... Railroad Av.
Hopper & Scott. Organzine and Tram. Hope Mill. Mill St.
Howell & Schoals. Lyons Silk Mill. Dress Goods,
 Handkerchiefs. Whitney & Matthews, Selling Agents,
 85 Leonard St., New York. Factory, Dock Mill.. Van Houten St.
Jackson, James. Manufacturer of Jacquard Machines,
 Compass Boards and Silk Machinery...Works, 18-20 Albion Av.
Jackson, Joseph. Thrown Silks. Factory, Grant Lo-
 comotive Works................................ Paterson
Jones, J. W. Dress Goods. Handkerchiefs........ Oak St.
Little, W. & Co. Totowa Mill. Dress Goods and
 Handkerchiefs. Whitney & Matthews, Selling
 Agents, 85 Leonard St., New York. Mill......... Kearney St.
Lockett, John. Handkerchiefs, Dress Goods, Scarfs
 and Millinery Silks. Whitney & Matthews, Selling
 Agents, 85 Leonard St., New York. Dale Mills.... Railroad Av.
Lucas, Samuel. Dress, Millinery and Tie Goods, etc.
 Factory, Washington Market Building............ Fair St.
Mackay, J. P. Dress and Millinery Goods, Handker-
 chiefs and Veilings. Salesroom, 89 Leonard St.,
 New York. Mill...........................60-66 Water St.
Meding, C. E. Ribbons. E. Oelbermann & Co.,
 57-63 Greene St., New York, Selling Agents.
 Granite Mill.................................. Paterson
Mills (late Todd & Mills). Plushes, Velvets, etc...51 Mechanic St.
McAlister, James & Co. Silk Throwsters. Empire
 Mill...............................cor. Green and Jackson Sts.
Mende, Alex. P. Silk Manufacturers' Supplies, Machi-
 nery, Dyestuffs and Ribbon Paper...............171 Market St.
Morlot, Geo. Silk Dyer. Office, 454 Broome St.,
 New York. Works.............32d St. and 10th Av., Paterson

Neuburger Braid Co. L. & H. Neuburger. Silk
Braids, Fancy Goods, Bindings and Raw Silk
Throwing on Commission. Salesrooms, 39 and 41
Walker St., New York. Mills.................... Paterson
New Jersey Silk Manufacturing Co. B. B. Clark, President; Wright Smith, Superintendent. Dress Silks.
Franklin Mill..................................... Mill St
Nightingale Bros. Fine Grades Handkerchiefs, Dress
Goods, Satins, Tie Silks, Tissues and Gauze. Lewis
Bros. & Co., 86–88 Worth St, New York, Selling
Agents. Boudinot Mill................. Straight St, Paterson
Nightingale, James, Jr. Dress Silks, Satins, Rhadamés,
Serges and Ottoman Damassé. John Stewart & Co.,
55 Mercer St., New York, Selling Agents. Factory,
Dale Mill...................................... Railroad Av.
Paterson Dyeing Association. Pierre Thonnerieux,
Manager. Silk Dyers. Works............ Mill St., opp. Ellison
Pelgram & Meyer. Ribbons and Dress Goods. Salesrooms, 57–59 Greene St., New York. Mills at Boonton, N. J., and cor. Temple and Matlock Sts....... Paterson
Pfeffer & Wels. Spun Silk. Pope's Mill........... Paterson
Phœnix Manufacturing Co. Albert Tilt, President
and Treasurer; John R. Curran, Secretary. Handkerchiefs, Brocades, Dress Goods, Fancy Ribbons
and Ties. Greeff & Co., 20–26 Greene St., New
York, Selling Agents. Mills at Paterson, N. J., and
Allentown, Pa. Principal mill, Phœnix Mill, Van
Houten St....................................... Paterson
Pioneer Silk Co. John Ryle, President. Tram, Organzine and Ribbons. Murray Mills.............. Mill St.
Pocachard, A. Dress Silks and Novelties. Charles
G. Landon & Co., 419–421 Broome St., New York,
Selling Agents. Factory, 173–177 Market St...... Paterson
Riley, Edward. Silk Dyer................. Murray Mill, Mill St.
Rogers, James H. Handkerchiefs and Dress Goods.. 78 Mill St.
Ryle, John C. & Co. Commission Silk Throwsters.
Central Silk Mill................................ Ellison St.
See & Sheehan. Silk Dyers. Office, 96 Grand St.,
New York. Works..................... Ellison St., Paterson
Sherratt Thomas. Dress Goods and Handkerchiefs. 60 Railroad Av.
Singleton, George. Tram, Organzine, Sewing Silk and
Machine Twist. Watson Mill.................. Railroad Av.

Smith, Wright. Ribbons and Umbrella Silks. Union
   Manufacturing Co.............................. River St.
Southworth Bros. Dress Goods and Handkerchiefs.
   Ammidown, Lane & Co., 87-89 Leonard St., New
   York, Selling Agents. Mills, Morton St........... Paterson
Spantor & Palmer. Throwsters.................... Watson Mill
Strange, William & Co. Silk Goods, Ribbons, Milli-
   nery and Dress Silks, Tram and Organzine. Sales-
   rooms, Strange & Bro., 96-98 Prince St., New York.
   Mills, Essex and Paterson Sts.................... Paterson
Straub, William. Silk Designing and Card Cutting.
   Office..34 Hamburgh Av
Thorpe, Samuel. Commission Throwster......... Granite Mill
Todd & Mills. Silk Plushes and Velvets..........51 Mechanic St.
Townsend, Thomas. Handkerchiefs and Dress Goods.
   Barnet Mill............................... .... Railroad Av.
Urbahn, A. Ribbons.......................... .... 93 River St.
Vacher, Jerome. Dress Silks........................... 93 River St.
Walthall, James & Son. Floss and Embroidery Silks,
   Tram, Sewing Silk, Machine Twist and Saddlers'
   Heavy Canton Twist............................. 93 River St.
Weidmann, J. Silk Dyer. Office, 298 Canal St., New
   York. Works...................cor. Ellison and Paterson Sts.
Whitehead Bros. Handkerchiefs and Dress Goods.
   C. G. Landon & Co., 419-421 Broome St., New York,
   Selling Agents. Mill...................Railroad Av., Paterson
Whiteside, James & Co. Paul Crawford, Superintend-
   ent. Handkerchiefs, Scarfs and Dress Goods. Gros-
   venor & Carpenter, 54-56 White St., New York,
   Selling Agents........................Dale Mill, Railroad Av.
Winfield Manufacturing Co. Silk and Mohair Braids,
   Prussian Bindings, Galloons and Coat Hangers.
   John Stewart & Co., 55 Mercer St., New York,
   Selling Agents. Weaverton Mill..18th St. and 12th Av., Paterson

NEW JERSEY—(Continued).

Alexander, W. A. Silk Dyer. Near Warren St., Jersey City Heights
Bannigan, P. & I. Tram, Organzine, Fringe Silks,
   Ribbons and Satin Dress Goods. Salesroom, 68
   Greene St., New York. Mill..................... Lake View
Benedict, W. H. Laces, Hair Nets and Mitts. Of-

fice, 383 Broadway, New York. M. Drost, 18 Summer
St., Boston, Selling Agent. Factory and Salesroom. New Brunswick
Borelli, Joseph. Silk Dyer. Tonelle Av......Jersey City Heights
Chaffanjon, C. "Favorite" Silk Manufactory. Black
Gros-grain, Faille, Serges and Satin de Chine. Wilmerding, Hoguet & Co., 64-66 White St., New York,
Selling Agents. Mills, 177-189 South St.....Jersey City Heights
Chapperon, Louis. Dress Goods. Luckemeyer &
Schefer, 472 Broome St., New York, Selling Agents.
Mill..Town of Union
Clifton Silk Mills. F. Grossenbacher, Manager. Broad
Goods and Jacquard Silks. James McCreery & Co.,
803 Broadway, New York, Selling Agents. Mills.. Clifton
Clyde, E. H. Machine Twist. 22 Mechanic St..... Newark
Comby, John. Black and Colored Gros-grains. Salesroom, C. Passavant & Co., Agents, 222 Church St.,
New York. Mills, West St. and Paterson Av.,....West Hoboken
Cutter, John D. & Co. Sewing Silks, Machine Twist,
Gros-grain Dress Goods, Serges, Satin de Chine, and
Sewing Silk Braids. Salesrooms, 329-331 Broadway,
New York; 6 Bedford St., Boston; 735 Market St.,
Philadelphia; 127 Fifth Av., Chicago, and 26 New
Montgomery St., San Francisco. Newark City Silk Mills..Newark
Ehler, A. & B. Progress Mills. Dress Goods, Serges,
Satin de Chine........564-566 Palisade Av., Jersey City Heights
Englewood Silk Manufacturing Co. Throwsters........Englewood
Erskine, John & Co. Ribbons. Salesroom, 52 Greene
St., New York. Factory........................ Union Hill
ield, Morris, Church & Co. Plain, Black and Colored
Silks. Salesrooms, 74 Leonard St., New York. Factory.....cor. of Columbia and Lincoln Sts., Jersey City Heights
Gelan, C. Rhadamés and Ottoman Silks............ Union Hill
Givernaud Bros. Black and Colored Dress Silks,
Serges, Satin de Lyon, Damassés, Satins and Armures. Office, 46 Howard St., New York. Mills,
West Hoboken, Homestead and Hackensack
Hemburg, William. Silk Dyer.....................Midland Park
Hulsemann, John F. Essex Silk Mills. Machine
Twist. 20-22 Mechanic St...................... Newark
Jourdeuil & Pinkney. Dress Silks, Serges and Satin
de Chine. Salesroom, 123 Mercer St., New York.
Mills, West St. and Paterson Av................West Hoboken

Kamp, M. & C. Dress Goods. Post-office, Weehawken.
Concordia Mill, 19–24 Bloom St................Town of Union
Kluessner, Andrew. Steam Silk Works............West Hoboken
Laubsch, Charles. Brocades, Plain Dress Goods and
Neck-wear Silks. Post-office, Weehawken. Factory,
corner of Palisade Av. and Columbia St........... Union Hill
Meyenberg, S. M. Millinery, Dress and Tie Silks,
Scarfs, Ribbons, etc. Salesroom, 461 Broome St.,
New York. Factory............................. Hoboken
Pages, J. B. Silk Dyer. 99–101 Adams St.......... Hoboken
Pelgram & Meyer. Paterson, N. J. Mill at......... Boonton
Perks, George A. & Co. Upholstery Trimmings. Sales-
rooms, 39–41 North 3d St., Philadelphia, Mill.... Camden
Phalanx Silk Weaving Co. F. Traenkle, President;
J. C. Schlachter, Secretary; J. R. Waters, Treas-
urer; A. Teste, Superintendent. Dress Silks. Me-
groz, Portier, Grose & Co., 85–87 Grand St., New
York, Selling Agents. Factory..................West Hoboken
Phipps & Train. Spun Silk, Silk Noils, Noil Yarn.
Salesroom, 73 Leonard St., New York. Factory... Lakewood
Poidebard Silk Manufacturing Co. A. Poidebard,
President; G. Bierwirth, Treasurer; P. Ulrich,
Secretary. Capital, $75,000. Silk Dress Goods.
F. Vietor & Achelis, 66–72 Leonard St., New York,
Selling Agents. Factory........................North Bergen
Ratti, Joseph. Commission Silk Throwster. Th.
Cornu & H. Saillet, 49 Lispenard St., New York,
Selling Agents. Mill..........................West Hoboken
Rittenhouse Manufacturing Co. Tapestries......... Passaic
Simon, Herman. Dress Goods and Fancy Silks. E.
Oelbermann & Co., 57–63 Greene St., New York,
Selling Agents. Post-office, Weehawken. Factories,
Easton, Pa., and Garden and Morgan Sts........Town of Union
Singleton Manufacturing Co...................... Dover
Sonntag, H. Dress Trimmings, 219 Congress St., Jersey City Heights
Spangenberg, C., Jr. Upholstery Trimmings. Fac-
tory and Salesroom, 221 Park Av................ Hoboken
Wortendyke Manufacturing Co. C. A. Wortendyke,
President and Treasurer. Tram, Organzine, Dress
Goods and Handkerchiefs. Ammidown, Lane &
Co., 87–89 Leonard St., New York, Selling Agents.
Brick Mill..................................... Wortendyke

NEW YORK CITY.

Ackerman, W. C. Upholstery Trimmings...........233 Sixth Av.
Adams, R. & Co. (See *Paterson, N. J.*) Salesroom..10 Greene St.
Adams, R. & H. (See *Paterson, N. J.*) Salesroom, 83-85 Greene St.
Alcock, F. W. (See *Paterson, N. J.*) Salesroom of
  Selling Agents................................85 Leonard St.
Anderson, John & Sons. (See *Paterson, N. J.*) Salesroom of Selling Agent....................108-110 Franklin St.
Ashley & Bailey. (See *Paterson, N. J.*) Salesrooms
  of Selling Agents........................457-459 Broome St.
American Silk Label Manufacturing Co. George Hey, Manager. Silk Labels and Coat Hangers. Agencies at Boston, Chicago, Cincinnati, Philadelphia and St. Louis. Salesroom and Factory..........389 Broome St.
Aub, Hackenburg & Co. (See *Philadelphia, Pa.*) Salesroom..526 Broadway
Auerbach & Co. (See *Paterson, N. J.*) Salesroom, 526 Broadway
Bannigan, P. & I. (See *Lake View, N. J.*) Salesroom, 68 Greene St.
Barnard, O. H. Undertakers' Trimmings. Factory
  and Salesroom........................511-513 West 30th St.
Beierstedt, Carl. Upholstery Trimmings............138 Canal St.
Belding Bros. & Co. (See *Rockville, Conn.*) Salesroom, 456 Broadway
Bernstein, A. Millinery and Dress Trimmings..1680 Lexington Av.
Bernstein, Samuel. Fringes, Dress Trimmings, etc...91 Bleecker St.
Bernstein & Co. Cords, Tassels and Specialties....133 Mercer St.
Bertschy, Samuel. Ribbons and Novelties..........625 Tenth Av.
Betts, Jacob. Silk Braids.....................519 West 45th St.
Blau, Max. Dress, Cloak and Fur Trimmings.......51 Greene St.
Bodmer, Edward. Silk Dyer..................404 West 50th St.
Boesen, Pauline. Fringes and Passementerie........29 Mercer St.
Boettger, Hinze & Kueppers. Finishing of Broad Silks
  and Satins..47 Mercer St.
Bomann, Joseph. (See *Brooklyn.*) Office...........8 Greene St.
Booth, J. H. & Co. (See *Paterson, N. J.*) Salesroom, 54 Howard St.
Boston Elastic Fabric Co. (See *Chelsea, Mass.*) Salesroom..332 Broadway
Bottum & Trescott. (See *Springfield, Mass.*) Salesroom, 55 Walker St.
Brainerd & Armstrong Co. (See *New London, Conn.*)
  Salesroom..469 Broadway
Bromly, J. & Son. (See *Philadelphia, Pa.*) Salesroom
  of Selling Agent....................................317 Broadway
Broomhall, Geo. L. (See *Paterson, N. J.*) Salesroom
  of Selling Agents....................................85 Leonard St.

Brown, Edward G.   Upholstery Trimmings.....787-789 Broadway
Brown, George W.   Dress Trimmings.............403 Broadway
Brown, L. D. & Son.   (See *Middletown, Conn.*)   Salesroom..439 Broadway
Brown, William P.   Ribbons.   Iselin, Neeser & Co.,
   Selling Agents, 339 Canal St.   Mill......457-463 West 45th St.
Buschmann, C. H.   Fringes, Dress Trimmings, Cords
   and Tassels...................................36 East 14th St.
Butler, H. V., Jr., & Co.   Silk Ribbon Paper.   General Agents for the Ivanhoe Manufacturing Co..... 32 Reade St.
Camp, John T. & Co.   Trimmings, Fringes, Cords and
   Tassels.   Factory and Salesroom..................19 Mercer St.
Chaffanjon, C.   (See *Jersey City Heights, N. J.*)   Salesroom of Selling Agents....................64-66 White St.
Chapperon, Louis.   (See *Town of Union, N. J.*)   Salesroom of Selling Agents.........................472 Broome St.
Chapin, J. L.   (See *Paterson, N. J.*)   Office......... 96 Reade St.
Cheney Bros.   (See *South Manchester, Conn.*)   Salesrooms..477-481 Broome St.
City Button Works.   Erlanger & Liebman, Proprietors.   Silk and Crochet Buttons.   Factory, 116 Walker St.   Office............................. 238 Canal St.
Clark, R. S.   (See *Mount Carmel, Conn.*)   Salesroom of Selling Agent................................327 Broadway
Clifton Silk Mills.   (See *Clifton, N. J.*)   Salesroom of Selling Agents....................................803 Broadway
Collet, A. & Co.   Upholstery Trimmings............900 Broadway
Comby, John.   (See *West Hoboken, N. J.*)   Salesroom of Selling Agents................................222 Church St.
Copcutt, William H. & Co.   (See *Yonkers, N. Y.*)   Salesrooms of Selling Agents..............457-459 Broome St.
Crosley, C. W.   Cloak and Dress Trimmings........920 Broadway
Cutter, John D. & Co.   (See *Newark, N. J.*)   Salesrooms...329-331 Broadway
Dale, Frederick S.   (See *Paterson, N. J.*)   Salesrooms of Selling Agents............................419-421 Broadway
Dalton, Joseph.   Hair Nets, Laces and Canvas.
   Agencies at Boston and Chicago.   Factory..108-110 Wooster St.
Dean, Henry.   Fringes and Furniture Trimmings, 54-60 West 16th St.
Deppeler & Kammerer.   Fringes and Dress Trimmings. 108 Grand St.
Dexter, Lambert & Co.   (See *Paterson, N. J.*)   Salesrooms...33-35 Greene St.

Dietzel & Green. Millinery and Fancy Trimmings.
Factory, 398 Broome St., New York. Agency, 28
Rue de Trévise, Paris. Salesroom (about to move
from)..534 Broadway
Doherty & Wadsworth. (See *Paterson, N. J.*) Sales-
rooms of Selling Agents......................85–87 Grand St.
Downs & Adams. (See *Athol, Mass.*) Salesroom....48 Walker St.
Dreyfus Bros. Fringes, Upholstery Trimmings and
Passementerie. Factory and Salesroom.........52 Lispenard St.
Dreyfus & Hecht. Dress Trimmings..............107 Greene St.
Dunlop, John. (See *Paterson, N. J.*) Salesroom.,..25 Mercer St.
Eicke, Edward. Military and Schutzen Trimmings...157 Canal St.
Ellison, Adolph S. Fringes, Passementerie, Cords,
Tassels, Chenille, Buttons and Novelties.....103–105 Greene St.
Elwood, B. H. & Co. (See *Fort Plain, N. Y.*) Sales-
room of Selling Agents........................55 Mercer St.
Ennis, Geo. W. & Co. (*Philadelphia, Pa.*) Sales-
room of Selling Agents........................64–66 White St.
Erskine, John & Co. (See *Union Hill, N. J.*) Sales-
room...52 Greene St.
Eschbach, S. & Son. Silk Dyer................348 West 44th St.
Eureka Silk Manufacturing Co. (See *Canton, Mass.*)
Salesroom....................................... 7 Mercer St.
Fessler, Henry. Cigar Ribbons, Galloons and Prussian
Bindings..................................343–345 West 37th St.
Field, Morris, Church & Co. (See *Jersey City Heights,
N. J.*) Salesroom..............................74 Leonard St.
Fisher, C. Dress Trimmings......................8 Howard St.
Fisher, M. Dress Trimmings....................471 Broadway
Franke, Louis. (See *Paterson, N. J.*) Salesroom...110 Grand St.
Friend, Hermann. Trimmings and Passementerie....98 Greene St.
Funke, Hugo. (See *College Point, L. I., N. Y.*) Sales-
rooms.......................................23–25 Greene St.
Gartner & Friedenheit. Ribbons................. 89 Grand St.
Gehlert, Edward. Fringes, Dress Trimmings and Pas-
sementerie....................................2327 Fourth Av.
Givernaud Bros. (See *Hoboken, N. J.*) Salesroom..46 Howard St.
Glendale Elastic Fabric Co. (See *Easthampton, Mass.*)
Salesroom of Selling Agents....................8 Thomas St.
Glenwood Mills. (See *Easthampton, Mass.*) Salesroom
of Selling Agents.........................419–421 Broome St.
Glockmann, J. L. Gimps and Fringes.............21 Wooster St.

Gminder, Frederic & Co.   Fringes and Dress Trim-
   mings.   Agencies in Philadelphia and Chicago.
   Factory, 10th Av. and 45th St.   Salesroom........66 Greene St.
Godshalk, E. H.   (See *Philadelphia, Pa*) Salesroom.323 Broadway
Goodman, B.   Silk Webbing...................... 7 White St.
Gossage, Charles & Co.   (See *Chicago, Ill.*)   Salesroom
   of Selling Agents...................cor. Church and Worth Sts.
Graf, Jacob.   Embroidery by Hand and Machine...215 Church St.
Graham, John & Son.   Upholstery and Undertakers'
   Trimmings.   Factory and Salesroom.......516–524 W. 35th St.
Greenbaum, Louis & Son.   New York Cord and Tassel
   Mill.   Curtain Cords and Tassels.............65–67 Duane St.
Gregson & McCulloch.   (See *Paterson, N. J.*)   Sales-
   room of Selling Agents............................353 Canal St.
Greppo, Claude.   (See *Paterson, N. J.*)   Office......27 Mercer St.
Grimshaw Bros.   (See *Paterson, N. J.*)   Salesrooms
   of Selling Agents.............................57–63 Greene St.
Grish, John.   (See *Paterson, N. J.*)   Salesroom of
   Selling Agents..........54–56 White and 108–110 Franklin Sts.
Grollimund, J.   Cigar Ribbons..........cor. 19th St. and 11th Av.
Gross, Caspar.   Dress Trimmings..............523 West 45th St.
Hafelfinger, Fritz.   Fringes and Dress Trimmings, 343–345 W. 37th St.
Hafelfinger, Jacob.   Fringes and Dress Trimmings..444 W. 38th St.
Hafelfinger, John.   Dress Trimmings...............462 10th Av.
Hahn & Jaragzewski.   Dress Trimmings, Cords and
   Tassels..54 Lispenard St.
Hall, Thomas R.   Silk and Cotton Elastic Bandages..211 E. 22d St.
Hamil & Booth.   (See *Paterson, N. J.*) Salesrooms.96–98 Grand St.
Hammond & Knowlton.   (See *Putnam, Conn.*)   Sales-
   room..524 Broadway
Haraux & Co.   European Embroidering Co....146–148 Wooster St.
Harris & Klein.   Dress, Cloak and Millinery Trim-
   mings and Hat Cords........................ ...604 Broadway
Hartford Silk Manufacturing Co.   (See *Tariffville,
   Conn.*)   Salesroom of Selling Agents.............45 Leonard St.
Haskell Silk Co.   (See *Saccarappa, Me.*)   Salesroom
   of Selling Agents........................ ......36 Lispenard St.
Haubner, L. D.   Upholstery Trimmings.........153 West 46th St.
Hawks, M. J. & Co.   (See *Paterson, N. J.*)   Sales-
   room of Selling Agent...........................81 Greene St.
Hayes, Thomas F.   Fringes and Dress Trimmings.
   Factory and Salesroom............ ....5 to 9 Union Square

Heineman, Jacob. Dress Trimmings..............650 Broadway
Heidenreich, John. Silk Dyer..............543-545 Tenth Av.
Heminway, M. & Sons, Silk Co. (See *Watertown,
   Conn.*) Salesrooms............78 Reade St. and 99 Church St.
Hentze, Marcus. Upholstery Trimmings & Fringes. 7 Washington Pl.
Hertlein & Schlatter. Fringes and Dress Trimmings.
   Factory and Office.............................26 Greene St.
Hess, Isaac. Dress and Cloak Trimmings, Fringes,
   Cords and Tassels..............................5 Howard St.
Hirsch, Isaac. Dress Trimmings and Silk Fringes..7 Washington Pl.
Hirsh, M. & Son. Dress Trimmings & Passementerie, 420 Broome St.
Hofmann & Ellrodt. Millinery, Trimmings, Braids,
   Cords and Tassels........................91 Mercer St.
Holland Manufacturing Co. (See *Willimantic, Conn.*)
   Salesrooms...................................435 Broadway.
Horn, Henriette. Ribbons..............445-447 West 42d St.
Horstmann, Wm. H. & Sons. (See *Philadelphia, Pa.*)
   Salesroom....................................106 Grand St.
Howard, E. & S. Silk Veiling ....511 West 42d St.
Howard, George. Millinery Silks............404 West 33d St.
Howell & Schoals. (See *Paterson, N. J.*) Salesrooms. 85 Leonard St.
Itschner, (Werner) & Co. (See *Philadelphia, Pa.*)
   Salesroom....................................70 Mercer St.
Jennings, A. G. (See *Brooklyn, N. Y.*) Salesroom, 473-475 Broome St.
Jourdeuil & Pinkney. (See *West Hoboken, N. J.*)
   Salesroom...................................123 Mercer St.
Judson, Charles. Webs and Suspenders...........73 Leonard St.
Kammerer & Bockstoever. Fringes, Dress Trimmings,
   Cords and Tassels.... ....111 Greene St.
Kelty, G. L. & Co. (See *Brooklyn, N. Y.*) Salesroom..831 Broadway
Kimball, W. E. Silk Spooling and Winding.........168 Centre St.
Klotz, Herman. Silk and Half-Silk Coat Hangers..22 Eldridge St.
Krause & Karbach. Embossers and Printers on Silks,
   Velvets and Plushes; also Ribbon Watering.....138 Wooster St.
Krumsick, Rudolph. Fringes and Dress Trimmings. 29 Howard St.
Kunz, Samuel. Ribbons............ ....413 East 25th St.
Kursheedt Manufacturing Co. Laces, Embroideries,
   Quiltings, Trimmings, etc. Salesrooms, 69-71 Greene
   St., New York, and 87-89 Wabash Av., Chicago, Ills.
   Factories, South 5th Av., Thompson St. and West
   19th St, New York. Counting Room, Order and
   Shipping Departments.....................194 South 5th Av.

Langlotz, Louis. Dress and Cloak Trimmings. 441-443 West 42d St.
Lauderbach & Daggett. (See *New Haven, Conn.*)
 Salesroom..472 Broadway
Laurent, Eugene. Needle-wrought Silk Buttons. 225 East 125th St.
Leiter, I. H. Upholstery Trimmings and Gimps..210-212 Canal St.
Leonard Silk Co. (See *Warehouse Point, Conn.*) Salesroom..140 Church St.
Leschhorn, F. & Co. Dress and Cloak Trimmings, Cords, Tassels, Chenilles and Buttons............21 Howard St.
Liebermuth, A. & Co. Fringes and Dress Trimmings..69 Mercer St.
Lindenthal Bros. Upholstery and Drapery Trimmings.
 Agency, Boston. Factory and Office........739-741 Broadway.
Lipper, M. W. & Co. (See *Philadelphia.*) Salesroom..77 Franklin S*
Lips, Joseph. Lyons and Crefelder Silk Refinishing Establishment......................141 West Broadway.
Little, William & Co. (See *Paterson, N. J.*) Salesroom of Selling Agents..................85 Leonard St.
Lobenstein, S. Upholstery Trimmings............38 East 14th St.
Lockett, John. (See *Paterson, N. J.*) Salesroom of Selling Agents........................85 Leonard St.
Loewenstine & Kayser. (See *Brooklyn, N. Y.*) Salesroom..187 Church St.
Loth, Joseph & Co. Fine Silk Ribbons. Factory, 517 to 523 West 45th St. Salesroom................458 Broome St.
Lowenstein, J. & Co. Fringes, Cords and Passementerie, 85 Walker St.
Macfarlane, James S. (See *Mansfield Centre, Conn.*)
 Salesroom..24 Walker St.
Mackay, J. P. (See *Paterson, N. J.*) Salesroom...89 Leonard St.
Matter, John. Silk Dyer ....333 West 44th St.
Maidhof, J. Fringes and Dress Trimmings, Cords, Tassels and Chenille Fringes. Agencies, Philadelphia, Chicago and San Francisco. Factory and Salesroom, 401 Broadway
Mandel, Henry. Dress Trimmings, Braids, Cords and Molds..114 Centre St.
Martin, Charles N. Sewing Silk and Twist..........350 Canal St.
Maul, Hugo & Co. Dress Trimmings...... ...718-720 Broadway
McNaught & Co. Glasgow Printing Co. Printing on Silks, etc....................................107 Walker St.
Meding, E. (See *Paterson, N. J.*) Salesroom of Selling Agents.....................................57-63 Greene St.
Menges, A. Dress and Cloak Trimmings.......644-646 Broadway
Meyenberg, S. M. (See *Hoboken, N. J.*) Salesroom..461 Broome St.

SILK GOODS DIRECTORY.—NEW YORK CITY. 129

Meyer, G. L. & Co.   Upholstery Trimmings.......424 Broome St.
Moeller, Frederick.   Yarns......................428 Broome St.
Morlot, George.   (See *Paterson, N. J.*)   Office.....454 Broome St.
Morrison, James.   Dress and Cloak Trimmings......28 Howard St.
Müller, Ernst.   Millinery Trimmings...............127 Grand St.
Murray, Russell.   Dealer in Organzine and Tram, and
   English and Domestic Cotton Yarns..............52 Greene St.
National Suspender Co....................447-453 West 26th St.
Neuburger Braid Co.   (See *Paterson, N. J.*)   Sales
   rooms..................... ....39-41 Walker St.
Neustaedter, William.   Dealer in Tram, Organzine and
   Spun Silk......................................83 Mercer St.
New, Jacob.   Ribbons.   Factories, 529-533 West 54th,
   and 522-526 West 55th Sts.   Salesrooms......109-113 Grand St.
New York Woven Label Manufacturing Co.   Wm. Fried-
   hof, Woven Silk Labels, Hangers and Badges.   Fac-
   tory and Office..... ....52 Mercer St.
Nightingale Bros.   (See *Paterson, N. J.*)   Office.....339 Broadway
Nightingale, James, Jr.   (See *Paterson, N. J.*)   Sales-
   room of Selling Agents...........................55 Mercer St.
Nonotuck Silk Co.   (See *Florence, Mass.*)   Salesroom, 19 Mercer St.
Nordheim & Deimel.   Upholstery Trimmings.......734 Broadway
Novelty Silk Works.   Klous & Co.   Silk Novelties.
   Factory, 445-447 West 42d St.   Salesroom.......113 Mercer St.
O'Brien, Maurice.   Worsted, Worsted and Silk, and
   Silk Upholstery Trimmings.... ....90-92 Bowery
Oneida Community.   (See *Community, N. Y.*)   Thomas
   Handy, Agent.   Salesroom.......... ....53 Walker St.
Paine, Byrne & Co.   Lace Dyeing and Ribbon Watering, 9 Walker St.
Patterson, Erbacher & Co.   (See *Bridgeport, Conn.*)
   Salesroom ....75 Greene St.
Pelgram & Meyer.   (See *Paterson, N. J.*)   Salesrooms, 58-60 Greene St.
Phalanx Silk Weaving Co.   (See *West Hoboken, N. J.*)
   Salesroom of Selling Agents.... ....85-87 Grand St.
Phillips, A. L. & Co.   Cloak, Furriers' and Hatters'
   Trimmings.   Factory and Salesroom............ 121 Spring St.
Phipps & Train.   (See *Lakewood, N. J.*)   Salesroom, 73 Leonard St.
Phœnix Manufacturing Co.   (See *Paterson, N. J.*)
   Salesrooms............................. ....20-26 Greene St.
Piek, S.   Fringes and Cloak Trimmings.   Iselin,
   Neeser & Co., Selling Agents, 339 Canal St.   Fac-
   tory ......·..............cor. South 5th Av. and Bleecker St.

Pocachard, A. (See *Paterson, N. J.*) Salesroom of
  Selling Agents.................................419–421 Broome St.
Poidebard Silk Manufacturing Co. (See *North Bergen,
  N. J.*) Salesroom of Selling Agents.........66–72 Leonard St.
Popper, Isadore. Dress Trimmings...............25 Howard St.
Prosnitz & Salzer. Cords, Ornaments and Tassels...643 Broadway
Puttfarcken, E. Dress and Cloak Trimmings, Cords
  and Tassels..................................136–138 Greene St.
Ratti, Joseph. (See *West Hoboken, N. J.*) Salesroom
  of Selling Agents.............................49 Lispenard St.
Rauch, John. Novelty Embroidery Co. Embroideries
  by Hand and Machine.........................153 Walker St.
Reitmeyer & Co. (See *Brooklyn, N. Y.*) Salesroom..260 Canal St.
Reshower, Joseph & Co. Dress Trimmings, Fringes
  and Ornaments................................3 East 4th St.
Richmond Silk Manufacturing Co. Geo. Richmond,
  President; L. P. Williams, Treasurer. Serges, Dress
  Goods and Coat Linings. Factory, 445–447 West
  42d St. Salesroom...........................113 Mercer St.
Rockwell, Charles B. (See *Brooklyn, N. Y.*) Office...56 Reade St.
Roggwiller, Ed. Swiss Embroidery..................8 Walker St.
Romann, William. Cords and Tassels..............147 Spring St.
Ryer & Wagner. Upholstery Trimmings, Frame Fringes,
  Tassels, Cords and Curtain Loops............167–169 Canal St.
Sacks & Bro. Silk Fringes.......................34 Greene St.
Salathe, I. & M. Dress Trimmings.............170–172 Centre St.
Sandmann, Philip. Furriers' Dress and Cloak Trimmings, 263 Bowery
Sauquoit Silk Manufacturing Co. (See *Sauquoit, N. Y.*)
  Salesroom.....................................54 Howard St.
Schloss, H. & Co. Castle Braid Co. Mohair and Silk
  Braids and Millinery Novelties..............495–509 1st Av.
Schmadeke, F. W. & Co. Dress and Cloak Trimmings, 8 E. 14th St.
Schmid, Francis J. Coach Laces and Carriage Trim-
  mings. Factory and Salesroom..................5 West 4th St.
Schmidt, C. A. Drapery and Upholstery Trimmings.
  Factory and Salesroom....83–85 Chambers, and 65–67 Reade St.
Schmutz, Martin. Dress and Millinery Trimmings..504 W. 45th St.
Schnitzler, B. Cords and Tassels..................639 Broadway
Schwensen, Wm. Fringes, Dress Trimmings, Chenille,
  Cords, Tassels and Ornaments. Agencies at Boston
  and Chicago. Factory and Salesroom.........15–17 Mercer St.
Seavey, Foster & Bowman. (See *Eureka Silk Manu-
  facturing Co., Canton, Mass.*) Salesroom..........7 Mercer St.

See & Sheehan. (See *Paterson, N. J.*) Office.......96 Grand St.
Selling, H. & Co. Undertakers' Supplies.......105-111 Crosby St.
Silbermann, J. & Co. Bonnet and Belt Ribbons, Dress Trimmings, Silk Handkerchiefs and Piece Goods. Factories, 452-456 Tenth Av., and at Main St., Poughkeepsie. Salesroom.......................35 Mercer St.
Silberstein & Mayer. Furriers' Trimmings.........115 Mercer St.
Simon, Herman. (See *Weehawken, N. J.*) Salesrooms....................................57-63 Greene St.
Skinner, Geo. B. & Co. (See *Yonkers, N. Y.*) Salesroom, 27 Mercer St.
Skinner, Wm. & Son. (See *Holyoke, Mass.*) Salesroom, 508 B'way.
Smith, E. B. (See *Gurleyville, Conn.*) Salesroom of Selling Agents....................................456 Broadway
Smith & Rush. Bullion, Fancy and Chenille Fringes, Gimps, Cords, Tassels, etc..............105-107 East 13th St.
Southworth Bros. (See *Paterson, N. J.*) Salesrooms of Selling Agents.........................87-89 Leonard St.
Splitdorf, Henry. Silk Covering to Telegraph Wire..176 Worth St.
Springer, R. & Co. Dealers in Tram and Twist....464 Broome St.
Stanton Brothers. Commission Merchants and Manufacturers of Silk and Lace Novelties..............51 Greene St.
Stearns, John N. & Co. Black and Colored Gros-Grain Silks, Brocaded Dress Silks, Plain and Fancy Handkerchiefs. Factories, 213-221 East 42d St. and 214-224 East 43d St. Salesroom...............458 Broome St.
Steinhardt, A. Cords and Tassels..........121-123 South 5th Av.
Stepath, Charles. Dress and Cloak Trimmings, Fringes, Cords and Tassels.............................30 Howard St.
Stiffsonn, S. J. Bullion, Fancy and Chenille Fringes, Borders, Galloons, Gimps, Cords and Tassels...111 East 11th St.
Strange, William & Co. (See *Paterson, N. J.*) Salesrooms of Selling Agents......................96-98 Prince St.
Straus, F. A. Cotton, Worsted and Silk Yarns......29 Howard St.
Streeter & Mayhew. (See *Shelburne Falls, Mass.*) Salesroom of Selling Agent................... ... 7 Mercer St.
Sutro Bros. Silk, Mohair, Cotton and Silk Braids, Tubular Braids and Hat Cords, Bow Ties, Fringe Braids and Braided Cords. Sole Manufacturers of Braids on Patent Cards. Agencies at Boston and Chicago. Factory and Salesroom..... .. ...35-37 Wooster St.
Teste & Co. (See *West Hoboken, N. J.*) Salesroom of Selling Agents............................85-87 Grand St.

Thalmann, N. Silk Ribbons and Hat Bands..441–443 West 42d St.
Thorp, James H. & Co. (See *Brooklyn*.) Salesrooms, 429 Broome St.
Thorp, Robert & Sons. Galloons, Prussian Bindings,
 Ribbons, Silk, Cotton and Mohair Braids..........52 Greene St.
Tingue, House & Co. Mohair, Genappe, Worsted, Cotton and Spun Silk Yarns .... 56 Reade St.
Turner, P. W. & Son. (See *Turnerville, Conn.*) Salesroom ....27 Greene St.
Ulmer & Pauer Silk Dyers....................13–17 Crosby St.
Union Braiding Works. John Henry Vogt. Silk Cotton and Worsted Braids, Dress and Millinery Trimmings and Novelties...270 Bowery, bet. Prince and Houston Sts.
Van Liew, H. A. Dress Goods. Factory, 617 West 39th St. H. B. Claflin & Co., Selling Agents.....140 Church St.
Vickers & Weston. (See *Philadelphia, Pa.*) Salesroom, 62 White St.
Walter, Richard. Organzine, Tram and Ribbons. Mills, 456–458 W. 46th St. Salesroom of Selling Agents, 222–224 Church St.
Webendorfer, H. Cords, Fringes, Tassels and Trimmings................................... 288 Bowery
Weidmann, J. (See *Paterson, N. J.*) Office........298 Canal St.
Weil Bros. Dress and Cloak Trimmings............75 Greene St.
Weinberg, C. & Co. Upholstery and Drapery Trimmings ....740–742 Broadway
Weiss, William. Fringes and Dress Trimmings......506 Broadway
Wherlin, M. & Co. Silk Dyers.......... .. 341–343 East 29th St.
Whitehead Bros. (See *Paterson, N. J.*) Salesroom of Selling Agents...........................419–421 Broome St.
Whiteside, James & Co. (See *Paterson, N. J.*) Salesroom of Selling Agents........................54–56 White St.
Wicke, William & Co. Cigar Ribbons..........Goerck and 3d Sts.
Winfield Manufacturing Co. (See *Paterson, N. J.*)
 Salesroom of Selling Agents..................... 55 Mercer St.
Williams, P. H. & W. Silk and Worsted Upholstery Trimmings...................................145–147 Fifth Av.
Wimpfheimer & Bassett. Dress Trimmings.........106 Greene St.
Woodruff Bro. & Beardsley. (See *Auburn, N. Y.*)
 Salesroom of Selling Agents....................85 Leonard St.
Wortendyke Manufacturing Co. (See *Wortendyke, N. J.*)
 Salesroom of Selling Agents.................87–89 Leonard St.
Zaisser, William. Silk Dyer................333–335 West 52d St.

BROOKLYN.

Bomann, Joseph. Dress and Cloak Trimmings. Office,
8 Greene St., New York. Factory.........828 Myrtle Av., Bkln.
Brooklyn Knitting Works. Chas. E. Hodge. Silk and
Woolen Knit Goods for Underwear.......106 Patchen Av., Bkln.
Estberg, E. Shade Tassels and Cords. Factory,
72-76 Hamburg Av., Bkln., E. D.
Halsey, A. Designing and Painting on Silk. Factory....................................287 Unio St., Bkln.
Jennings, A. G. Guipure, Thread, Blonde, Brussels
and Spanish Laces, Lace Mitts, Scarfs, Neck Ties and
Hair Nets. Salesrooms, 473-475 Broome St., N. Y.
Factory..."Jennings' Lace Works," Park Av. and Hall St., Bkln.
Kelty, G. L. & Co. Upholstery Trimmings, Furniture
Coverings and Curtain Materials, Cords, Gimps, Tassels and Fringes. Salesroom, 831 Broadway, New
York. Factory..................197-207 10th St., Bkln., E. D.
Loewenstine & Kayser. Silk Mitts, Laces, Scarfs and
Hair Nets. Salesroom, 187 Church St., New York,
Factory.......................20-32 Morton St., Bkln., E. D.
Maynard, A. & Co. Upholstery Trimmings, 100 S. 6th St., Bkln., E. D.
McLure, S. Upholstery and Dress Trimmings, Fringes,
Cords, Tassels and Gimps.................261 Fulton St., Bkln.
Moll, August. Braids..............146-152 First St., Bkln., E. D.
Naul, J. Cords and Braids..........128 Myrtle Av., Bkln., E. D.
Reitmeyer & Co. Fringes and Dress Trimmings. Salesroom, 260 Canal St., N. Y. Factory..17-27 S. 3d St., Bkln., E. D.
Rockwell, Charles B. Columbia Mills. Fancy Silk,
Mohair and Worsted Yarns. Office, 56 Reade St.,
New York. Factory............52-56 Columbia Heights, Bkln.
Soar, Henry G. H. Nottingham Laces and Hair Nets.
Factory......................So. 8th and 1st Sts., Bkln., E. D.
Steinborn, John D. German-American Braiding Works.
Dress Trimmings and Laces......57-59 Scholes St., Bkln., E. D.
Thorp, James H. & Co. Furniture Gimps. Salesroom,
429 Broome St., N. Y. Factory, cor. 4th and 5th Sts., Bkln., E. D.
Will, Jacob. Hat Cords...........357 South 3d St., Bkln., E. D.
Willes, Thomas. Marine Pictures in Silk. 188 Columbia St., Bkln.

NEW YORK STATE—(Continued).

Ashley & Bailey. (See *Paterson, N. J.*) Mill...... Fort Plain
Copcutt, William H. & Co. Ribbons, Handkerchiefs

and Piece Goods. A. Person, Harriman & Co., 457
and 459 Broome St., New York, Selling Agents.
Mills..............................Nepperhan Av.,   Yonkers
Elwood, B. H. & Co. Dress Goods and Handkerchiefs.
John Stewart & Co., 55 Mercer St., New York, Sell-
ing Agents. Mill............. ....   Fort Plain
Funke, Hugo. Ribbons, Organzine and Tram. Sales-
rooms, 23 and 25 Greene St., New York. Rhenania
Mills................................ ....College Point, L. I.
Gregson & McCulloch. (See *Paterson, N. J.*) Mill at Sloatsburg
Haiges, M. Dress, Upholstery and Decorative Trim-
mings. Factory, 401 Main and 9 Clinton Sts.
Office....................Room 46, Arcade Bldg.,   Buffalo
Hilton, Isaac. Dress Trimmings.......179 River St.,   Troy
Jewell & Bassett. Central City Ruffling and Lace
Goods. Factory..........43 to 47 Monroe Block,   Syracuse
Lacy, Lawrence. Lace Goods....48 South Salina St.,   Syracuse
Macfarlane, William. Nepperhan Silk Works. Thrown
Silk, Sewing Silk and Machine Twist..............   Yonkers
Nonotuck Silk Co. (See *Florence, Mass.*) Salesroom, Gloversville
Oneida Community (Limited). Sewing Silk and Ma-
chine Twist. Thomas Hardy, Salesman, 53 Walker
St., New York. Mills and General Office.........   Community
Sauquoit Silk Manufacturing Co. L. R. Stelle, Presi-
dent; Richard Rossmässler, Treasurer. Tram, Or-
ganzine and Fringe Silks. Factories, Sauquoit, near
Utica, N.Y.; Scranton, Pa., and Philadelphia. Sales-
rooms, cor. Columbia Av. and Randolph St., Phila-
delphia, and 54 Howard St., New York............   Sauquoit
Silbermann, J. & Co. (See *New York, N. Y.*) Main St., Poughkeepsie
Skinner, Geo. B. & Co. Tram, Organzine, Fringe Silk,
Sewing Silk and Machine Twist. Salesroom, 27 Mer-
cer St., New York. Mill ....   Yonkers
Vogt, Albrecht. Dress and Decorative Trimmings and
Casket Decorations. Factory...116 N. St. Paul St.,   Rochester
Roslyn Silk Manufacturing Co. Dumas & Taber.
Plain and Brocaded Dress Goods, Satins and Serges, Roslyn, L. I.
Woodruff Bro. & Beardsley. Piece Goods, Handker-
chiefs. Whitney & Matthews, 85 Leonard St., New
York, Selling Agents. Mill.....................   Auburn

OHIO.

Atkins, A.   Dress Trimmings.........102 W. 5th St.,   Cincinnati
Aub, Hackenburg & Co. (See *Philadelphia, Pa.*) Salesroom................................65 W. 3d St.,   Cincinnati
Bauer, Adolph.   Fringes and Dress Trimmings.   Factory and Salesroom..................142 W. 5th St.,   Cincinnati
Belding Bros. & Co.   (See *Rockville, Conn.*)   Salesroom................................136 Race St.,   Cincinnati
Broegelman, F.   Upholstery Trimmings.204 Vine St.,   Cincinnati
Franz, John.   Fringes and Upholstery Trimmings. Factory and Salesroom.............25 Oregon St.,   Cleveland
Hoffmeister, F.   Fringes and Passementerie.   Factory and Salesroom....................152 West 4th St.,   Cincinnati
Hoffmeister, Louis.   Fringes, Tassels, etc., 206 Vine St.,   Cincinnati
Mueller, Anton.....................7 East Pearl St.,   Cincinnati
Nonotuck Silk Co.   (See *Florence, Mass.*) Salesroom............................88 West 3d St.,   Cincinnati

---

PENNSYLVANIA.

PHILADELPHIA.

Alexander, Wm. B.   Cords, Gimps and Tassels.......16 N. 4th St.
Allen, W. P.   Raw and Spun Silk, Tassels and Fringes, 922 Howard St.
Aub, Hackenburg & Co.   Sewing Silk and Machine Twist.   Salesrooms : 20 N. 3d St., Philadelphia ; 526 Broadway, New York ; 19 Light St., Baltimore ; 65 W. 3d St., Cincinnati ; 152 5th Av., Chicago. Factory...........................244-248 N. Front St., Phila.
Barlow, Noah.   Upholstery, Raw and Spun Silks.   Factory........................53d St. and Westminster Av.
Belding Bros. & Co.   (See *Rockville, Conn.*)   G. W. Ellis, Manager.   Salesroom...............6th, cor. of Arch Sts.
Brainerd & Armstrong Co.   (See *New London, Conn.*) Salesroom....................................238 Market St.
Bromly, John & Sons.   Silk Upholstery, Carpets, Rugs, Hangings & Turcomans.   T. B. Shoaff, Selling Agent, 317 Broadway, New York.   Factory..Front and York Sts., Phila.
Bromly & Burns.   Dyers of Yarns and Silk Noils.
4026 Orchard St., Frankford
Brooks, Geo. & Son.   Upholstery and Furniture Covering,............................55th St. and Westminster Av.
Burnley, Joseph.............................1344 Columbia Av.

Courts, H. Dress Trimmings ....163 N. 2d St.
Coleman, William. Upholstery Trimmings..........25 N. 6th St.
Cunningham, W. B. Upholstery Trimmings........204 Church St.
Cutter, John D. & Co. (See *Newark, N. J.*) Salesroom, 735 Market St.
Davenport, George & Edwin. Upholstery Trimmings.
                       Susquehanna Av. and American St.
Davenport, H. Upholstery Trimmings.....Mascher and York Sts.
Davenport, John. Upholstery Goods. Somerset, Mascher & Norris Sts.
Ennis, George W. & Co. Upholstery Trimmings. Salesrooms, 64–66 White St., N. Y. Mill, Diamond & Howard Sts., Phila.
Fairhill Manufacturing Co. Silk Fringes and Tassels.
                       13th and Buttonwood Sts.
Forrest, John. Yarn Printing.............25th and Callowhill Sts.
Freyer, H. T. Dress Trimmings. Factory, 25 South 8th St. Salesroom............................727 Jayne St.
Godshalk, E. H. Fringes and Ladies' Dress Trimmings. Salesroom, 323 Broadway, New York. Factory....................cor. of 24th and Hamilton Sts., Phila.
Graham, J. C. Dress, Cloak and Upholstery Trimmings. Factory and Salesroom.................513 Cherry St.
Griswold Worsted Co. (Limited). (See *Darby, Pa.*)
   Office.......................................322 Chestnut St.
Hansell, S. R. & F. Upholstery Trimmings..........21 N. 4th St.
Harrison, Edwin. Upholstery Trimmings..........141 Master St.
Harrop, J. T. Sewing Silk and Machine Twist.....621 Market St
Hellwig & Spyr. Silk Dyers......................122 Eutaw St.
Heminway, M. & Sons Silk Co. (See *Watertown, Conn.*)
   Salesroom .... 14 N. 5th St.
Hensel, Colladay & Co. Dress Trimmings......7th St., near Arch.
Holland Manufacturing Co. (See *Willimantic, Conn.*)
   Salesroom..633 Market St.
Hooley, B. & Son. Tram, Twist and Fringe Silk.
   Mills......................................442–448 N. 13th St.
Horstmann, William H. & Sons. Gum Silks, Dress and Cloak Trimmings, Ribbons, Fringes, Floss, Upholstery Trimmings, Coach and Carriage Laces and Trimmings, Jacquard Weaving, Military Equipments, Regalia, Theatrical Goods, Silk Flags, Bunting, Sashes and Scarfs. Salesrooms, 106 Grand St., New York, and at Factory.....cor. of 5th and Cherry Sts., Phila.
Hovey, F. S. Sewing Silk and Machine Twist. ...248 Chestnut St.
Hoyle, Harrison & Kaye. Silk Upholstery Goods and Curtain Materials...................Lehigh Av. and Howard St.

Hunter, William & Son.   Upholstery Coverings and
   Tapestries.............................611-617 Dickenson St.
Itschner (Werner) & Co. Tioga Silk Mill. Ribbons and
   Hatbands. Salesrooms, 712 Market St., Philadelphia,
   and 70 Mercer St., New York. Mills, Tioga Station, Germantown
Jenkins, George E.   Upholstery Trimmings...........731 Filbert St.
Johnson, D. Waldo.   Sewing Silk and Machine Twist..323 Arch St.
Jones, T. & Son.   Silk Dyers......................110 Putnam St.
Kaufman, Strouse & Co. Scarfs, Ribbons, Fringes and
   Dress Trimmings. Salesroom..........cor. of 4th and Race Sts.
Kemper & McAuliffe. Fringes and Plush Trimmings..823 Market St.
Landenberger, Charles H......................1711 Randolph St.
Lazarus, Goldsmith & Co.   Chenille and Dress Trim-
   mings.............................12th and Buttonwood Sts.
Leonard Silk Co.   (See *Warehouse Point, Conn.*)   Sales-
   room..414 Arch St.
Lipper, M. W. & Co. Keystone Braid Mills. Dress
   Trimmings. Salesrooms, 144-146 N. 5th St., Phila-
   delphia ; 144 Wabash Av., Chicago, and 77 Franklin
   St., New York. Mills at.....................Wayne Station
Mabrey, Wm. H..................................414 Arch St.
Maurer, F. W. & Son. Manufacturers of Upholstery
   Trimmings....................................7-9 N. 5th St.
Montague and White. Ingrain Carpets, Woolen, Wor-
   sted and Silk Noil Yarns................Howard and Berks Sts.
Morell, Charles & Son. Silk Dyers............2219 Richmond St.
Mozieres, L. E. & P. Silk Dyers....................Philadelphia
Perks, George A. & Co.   (See *Camden, N. J.*)   Sales-
   rooms..39-41 N. 2d St.
Perry, Vincent. Silk Elastic Hosiery..48 Harvey St., Germantown
Revel, Justinian. Dress Goods and Trimmings.
                               55th St. and Wyalusing Av.
Ridgway, Edward. Upholstery Goods, 62d & Hamilton Sts., W. Phila.
Roehm, Joseph. Dealer in Sewing Silk and Twist....13 N. 4th St.
Rose, Charles. Cords, Dress Trimmings and Tassels..432 N. 3d St.
Sauquoit Silk Manufacturing Co. (See *Sauquoit, N. Y.*)
   Factory and Salesroom....cor. of Columbia Av. and Randolph St.
Schultheiss, E. Dress Trimmings and Fringes..3d and Poplar Sts.
Shrack & Sherwood. Dress and Upholstery Trimmings
   and Passementerie.........................231 Market St.
Stead & Miller   Upholstery Goods..........Coral and Adam Sts.
Sybert, Josiah B. Silk and Worsted Goods, Columbia Av., bel. 10th St.

Vickers & Weston. Cotton, Wool and Silk Hosiery. Agencies, Colladay, Trout & Co., 24–26 Bank St., Philadelphia, and 62 White St., New York. Factory .... Tulip and Palmer Sts., Phila.
Walliser, August. Fringes, Cords and Buttons...... 132 N. 8th St.
Walliser, Charles. Cords, Millinery Fringes and Passementeries .... 251 N. 8th St.
Woelpper Bros. Upholstery Trimmings...... Lehigh Av. and 3d St.

PENNSYLVANIA—(Continued).

Adelaide Silk Factory. Phœnix Manufacturing Co. (See *Paterson, N. J.*).............................. Allentown
Brainerd & Armstrong Co. (See *New London, Conn.*) Salesroom .... 4 Fifth Av., Pittsburg
Dexter, Lambert & Co. (See *Paterson, N. J.*) Bellemont and Nelson Mills....................... Hawley
Griswold Worsted Co. (Limited). Spun Silk. Office, 322 Chestnut St., Philadelphia. Mills at.......... Darby
Sauquoit Silk Manufacturing Co. (See *Sauquoit, N.Y.*) Mills at... Scranton
Simon, Herman. (See *Weehawken, N. J.*) Mill at.. Easton

UTAH TERRITORY.

Egbert, D. K. Dress Goods and Sewing Silk........ Kaysville
Utah Silk Association. Hon. Alex. C. Pyper, President and Superintendent; A. M. Musser, Secretary and Treasurer. Sewing Silk and Machine Twist. Factory and Office............................... Salt Lake City

VERMONT.

Stearns, J. F. Sewing Silk and Twist................ Brattleboro'

VIRGINIA.

Old Dominion Manufacturing Co. M. Umstadter, President. Embroideries......................... Norfolk

CANADA.

Belding, Paul & Co. Sewing Silk and Twist. (See *Rockville, Conn.*) Salesroom and Mill... 28–30 St. George St., Montreal

Canada **Silk Co.** A. M. Foster, President ; C. Bailis, Secretary and Treasurer ; Reuben Ryle, Manager. Sewing Silk, Machine Twist and Dress Goods...... Montreal

Corriveau Silk Mills Co. Plain and Brocaded Dress Silks, Handkerchiefs and Ribbons................ Montreal

Importers of Raw Silk.
NEW YORK CITY.

Arai, R., Representative of the Doshin Silk Co., Yokohama..18 Mercer St.
Auffm'Ordt, C. A. & Co........................33–35 Greene St.
Blydenburgh, Jesse S., Agent of **Walsh, Hall & Co.,** Yokohama... 66 Pine St.
Bourdis, J. & Co..51 Mercer St.
Bursley, Ira., Agent of Fraser, Farley & Co., Yokohama, 64 South St.
China and Japan Trading Co. (Limited)..34, 36 and 38 Burling Slip
Courian, Paul...109 Grand St.
Fearon, Low & Co., Shanghai. Agency............ 112 Front St.
Frazar & Co., of China. Agency.................... 74 South St.
Gibbes, A. H., Agent of Swire Bros., Shanghai....... 93 Wall St.
Hadden & Co... 109–111 Worth St.
Kai Oria, Agent of Yamato Trading Co., Japan......30 Howard St.
Lane, Geo. W. & Co.................107 Water and 93 Front Sts.
Low, A. A. & Bros...31 Burling Slip
Low, C. Adolphe & Co., Representatives of Ulysse Pila & Co., Lyons and Shanghai.................. 42 Cedar St.
Luckemeyer & Schefer ; also, Sole Agents of H. Ludwig & Co., Yokohama........................472–474 Broome St.
Ludwig, E., Agent of Arlès Dufour & Co., Lyons, 469–471 Broome St.
Milton, Wm. F. & Co..159 Maiden Lane
Morewood & Co..125 Front St.
Phillips, John C. & Co........................... 130 Water St.
Richardson, B. & Son, Agents for Durand, Badel & Huvey, Lyons and St. Etienne................... 5 Mercer St.
Russell & Co., Hong Kong and Shanghai. Office.... 59 Wall St.
Ryle, William ....54 Howard St.
Smith, Wm. H. & Son...77 William St.
Stoddard, Lovering & Co........................... 8 Thomas St.
Walker, John T., Son & Co. .. .. 81 Pine St.
Wetmore, Cryder & Co.............................73–74 South St.
Wood & Payson.. 64 Pine St.

Importers of Spun Silk.

Ryle, Wm., Agent of Lister & Co., Bradford, England, 54 Howard St.
Thairlwall, Wm. C.......... ....38 Lincoln St., Boston.
Wamsley, Philip & Co............................. 353 Canal St.

Brokers in Raw Silk.

Busch, P.... ....107 Grand St.
Cornu, Th. & H. Saillet..........................49 Lispenard St.
O'Donoghue & Co................................. 91 Grand St.
Hanssen, H. J.......................................34 Mercer St.
Haywood, Geo. M......... .... 39 White St.
Johnson, Rowland..... ....54 Beaver St.
Richardson, B. & Son............................. 5 Mercer St.
Simes, Charles F................................46 Howard St.
Smith, Isaac...................................... 4 Cedar St.

New York Silk Conditioning Works (Limited).

B. Richardson, President and Treasurer; L. Muzard,
General Manager............ ....13 Mercer St.

Women's Silk Culture Association.

Mrs. J. Lucas, President...........1328 Chestnut St., Philadelphia

www.ingramcontent.com/pod-product-compliance
Lightning Source LLC
Chambersburg PA
CBHW031334160426
43196CB00007B/686